Blending Families

MarriageToday
PO Box 59888
Dallas, TX 75229
1-800-868-8349

ISBN: 9780578176727

Ordering Information:
For sales details, contact the publisher at the address above.
Printed in the United States of America

Blending Families

18 Successful Stepfamilies Share Their Secrets to Growing a Healthy Marriage and Family

Jimmy Evans and Frank Martin

Contents

Before You Begin

Before you begin reading, we wanted to share a few thoughts on how to get the most out of this important resource.

When we set out to produce material to help people in blended families navigate the struggles and challenges that stepfamilies face, we wanted to do more than just write a book on the subject. We wanted to walk with families through the process as they work to make their marriage and family all that it can possibly be.

In order to accomplish this, we created an interactive workbook and study guide for couples and groups to be used along with this book. In the workbook, we included a teaching DVD that walks you through the 8-week study.

This teaching DVD includes candid interviews with the eighteen successful stepfamilies we brought together as our "panel of experts" when compiling material for this project. These are couples that have successfully navigated the unique challenges that blended families face—challenges that you may be facing on a daily basis.

Though this book can be read as a stand-alone resource, it is designed as a companion to the workbook and teaching DVD. Many of the thoughts and principles we discuss in the pages to come are developed further in the 8-week study.

Section one of this book is taken from Jimmy Evans' teaching on the "Day One Dynamics of a Blended Family." That complete teaching is included in the DVD that accompanies the workbook.

In section two of this book, we leaned heavily on the advice and counsel we received from the eighteen successful stepfamilies who agreed to help with this project. We included many direct quotes from those interviews in this section, but you'll find much more of their advice on the teaching DVD.

In section three, you'll find advice that applies to all married couples, blended or not, on growing a strong and healthy family.

If you are involved in a blended family Bible study or support group, we encourage you to look for these added resources and go through them with your group. If not, maybe you and your spouse can go through the workbook together as a couple.

Whatever you decide, our prayer is that God will use these resources to help you grow a strong and healthy, truly "blended" family.

To find these additional resources, visit our *Marriage Today* website, at www.marriagetoday.com

Chapter

When Two Become One ... Again

Brad and Pam have the kind of relationship that all married couples strive for. After thirty years of marriage, they still gaze at each other across the room with a knowing smile and a glint in their eyes. They finish each other's sentences and still flirt as they sit next to each other on the couch. Their speech is loving and respectful, especially when talking to each other. And you can tell from the moment you meet them how much in love they are.

It's hard to imagine Brad and Pam ever being in a bad marriage, yet that's exactly where they both once were—although not to each other.

Brad first married at the age of eighteen. "I got my girlfriend pregnant in high school and knew I needed to do the right thing," he said.

He wasn't a believer at the time, but he had the good character to take responsibility for his actions. So he married his girlfriend, and soon they were the parents of a beautiful baby boy. A couple years later they had a baby girl.

Brad always knew his girlfriend enjoyed "getting high" from time to time, but he never considered her an addict. It wasn't until after the wedding that he realized how serious the problem had become. She was good at hiding her drug habit, at least at first, but it wasn't long before she was getting high every day.

Brad also caught her cheating on him with other men—usually the ones who could help her to get hard drugs. And as the years went by, her addiction only grew worse.

"It was like being stuck in a washing machine set on the crazy cycle," Brad said. It was all he could do to try and maintain some semblance of normalcy for the sake of his kids. But the harder he tried to hang onto his family, the deeper she slid into the nightmare of drugs, sex, and emotional detachment.

The marriage didn't last long, and Brad's sole focus soon became fighting the courts for custody of his children. It was a constant uphill battle.

"At that time, judges always gave kids to the mother," he said. So he moved into a small apartment nearby and spent most of his time trying to protect his kids from their mother's destructive behavior.

Pam's first marriage wasn't any better. She married her boyfriend at the age of twenty-one, against the wishes of her parents. "It was the first rebellious thing I ever did," she remembers. He was charming and romantic, and quickly swept her off her feet. But he was also lazy, irresponsible, and sexually deviant. He never wanted to work, and when he did find jobs, he couldn't seem to keep them.

After six years of marriage they'd had two children—a boy and a girl—but still there was no stability in the family. "We were basically homeless for the first six years of our marriage," Pam said. "We bounced around from state to state, usually staying with friends."

Pam tried desperately to hold the family together, in spite of her husband's unwillingness to provide. But as time went on, his behavior only got worse. He became sexually abusive to Pam, and had a string of extramarital affairs.

"We went to seven different counselors in thirteen years of marriage," Pam said. Even in the midst of her husband's unfaithfulness, she wanted to stay together for the sake of the children. But it soon became clear that divorce was the only sane option.

"The man who mediated our divorce told me he had never seen anyone as mentally unstable as my first husband. He said he was like an emotional twelve-year-old."

So at the age of thirty-four, Pam became the single mother of two children. "I grew up in my first marriage," she says. "I can't regret it because the marriage gave me two beautiful children. And I learned how marriage is not supposed to work."

At times, the feelings of shame and grief felt overwhelming, but Pam never allowed herself to wallow in regret. She instead accepted her new reality, and threw her life into caring for her two precious children.

A Second Chance

Both Brad and Pam went into their second marriage with their eyes wide open. What they saw in each other was a chance to redeem the mistakes of their past, and build a healthy, happy marriage together, instead of a dysfunctional one.

"Brad was nothing like my first husband," says Pam. "I knew that he would be the kind of husband who gives. I didn't have that with my first marriage. I was the giver and he was the taker. I felt like I had finally found the man that I was supposed to be with. It just felt right."

Brad saw the same thing in Pam. "I quickly realized that this is how marriage is supposed to be."

And the one powerful thing that they both had in common was a commitment to make their second marriage last. "When we entered into our marriage, we said that divorce was never going to be an option for us," said Pam. "We would just learn to figure things out, no matter what problems came along."

Both Brad and Pam understood the challenges of going into marriage for a second time, and the inherent struggles that all stepfamilies face. They had four children between them, two ex-spouses who both wanted to play a role in their children's lives, the obligations of child support and past bills, and a lot of emotional wounds and baggage to navigate along the way. But these were challenges they were willing to face in order to have a secure and stable family.

This time, when challenges arose, they were committed to facing them head on. And they did all the right things in order to make things work. When money problems came and things started to get tight, they enrolled in a financial management course. When problems of discipline came up in their home, they began meeting regularly with a church pastor in order to learn new skills and techniques for stepfamilies. They joined small groups with other successful blended families, and learned all they could about what does and doesn't work when navigating a second marriage. At every opportunity they attended marriage classes and seminars at their local church in order to keep their marriage strong and their relationship on track. And they actively looked for older couples to mentor them in their marriage. In short, they began doing what all newly married couples should do in order to keep their love alive and thriving, and their family moving forward.

The Stats on Stepfamilies

Brad and Pam are living proof that blended families can work, in spite of the inherent struggles and challenges they face. Their story is encouraging, because it shows that remarriages can do much more than survive; they can actually thrive.

Marriage is challenging even under the best of circumstances. Some recent studies suggest that the divorce rate for first marriages is somewhere between thirty-eight to forty-two percent (far less than the fifty percent figure we've heard for years, but still not great odds). Those figures are significantly higher for remarriages, but they don't have to be. And that is one of our main purposes for writing this book. We want to give every blended family couple the knowledge, skills, and tools they need—not just to survive, but to thrive. Regardless of the statistics, every stepfamily can succeed.

Today, about half of all families are blended families. And they deal with some unique challenges that non-blended families don't have to navigate. Most often there is a history of pain and disappointment. There are likely feelings of guilt, shame, or regret. There are ex-spouses in the picture, and financial obligations already in place. And most often there are precious children caught in the middle of it all, struggling with a lot of the same emotions that their parents are fighting to overcome. The dynamics can feel overwhelming, especially to those who go into the relationship unequipped and unprepared.

Finding Hope

I (Jimmy) have been writing and teaching on marriage and family issues for most of my adult life, and if there's one truth I hold dear, it's that any marriage, no matter how strained or difficult it may feel, can go on to succeed wildly. With the right tools and attitude, any couple can overcome the many obstacles thrown in their path—including the special challenges brought on by a blended marriage.

Perhaps you're part of a blended family and struggling to make things work. Maybe you're having trouble connecting with a stepchild, or getting your own children to accept their new mom or dad. Or maybe your new marriage is taking a back seat to the demands of work, bills, and family, and you're looking for some concrete words of advice or support.

Maybe your situation is even more desperate. Perhaps you entered into a blended marriage assuming that things would work out, but now find that it's all you can do to get through the day without another family crisis or blowout with your new spouse. Your kids would rather spend time with your ex, and your stepchildren won't have anything to do with you. And your new wife or husband seems to take everyone's side but yours. You thought you were prepared for the challenges to come, but now that the honeymoon is over, your new blended family is anything but "blended."

If any of this rings true for you, then we encourage you to stay with us as we explore this subject together. In the pages to come, you'll find a wealth of great advice and counsel on issues that challenge stepfamilies on a daily basis.

Our "Panel of Experts"

When our staff at *Marriage Today* set out to create a comprehensive set of resources and curriculum for blended families, we had no desire to simply write another book on the subject. We wanted to create the most hands-on, realistic, no-nonsense set of tools we could possibly produce. We wanted to give advice that was solid, credible, and proven—and achievable for everyone.

Our goal was twofold:

First, we wanted to give practical, tried and true advice on overcoming the inherent "day one" dynamics of a blended family. These are specific challenges that exist at the very beginning of creating a stepfamily. And secondly, we wanted to address the special challenges and issues that can happen throughout the changing seasons of life and marriage in your blended family.

And our strategy for accomplishing these goals was to look to those who have already navigated those waters successfully. Experience is always the best coach and mentor, so when trying to blend two families into one, the best place to look for advice is from those who have succeeded in doing just that.

So we began by bringing together eighteen of the most successful blended families we could find. We looked for couples from all walks of life, from different cities and cultures, and at all stages of blended family life. We recruited couples of different ages and backgrounds, each with their own unique sets of challenges and circumstances. Couples who had been through the fire—some several times over—yet come out the other side intact and healthy and still going strong. We looked for couples who had succeeded in overcoming the struggles and obstacles that you're likely facing, or will face at some point in the future.

Couples like Brad and Pam, who never imagined themselves having to face the trials of a second marriage, but when confronted with the challenge, decided to tackle the task head on, and do whatever they needed to do in order to make things work.

We set out to find healthy and happy blended families who had effectively turned struggles into opportunities for growth. And who welcomed the chance to share what they had learned with others in their same situation.

These couples became our "panel of experts"—the ones that we looked to for workable strategies and advice on growing a strong blended family. And the wealth of wisdom and knowledge they brought to the table surpassed even our greatest expectations. They addressed issues that we didn't even know were issues among today's stepfamilies. And in the end, they helped us create this book for blended families that is far more helpful and insightful than we could have put together on our own.

Defining a Blended Family

So what constitutes a blended family? Before we get further along, let's take some time to define the families and people we had in mind when creating this unique set of resources for stepfamilies. Like all families, blended marriages come in lots of different shapes and makeups, but the simple definition we've chosen to use is any family unit where one or both parents come into the marriage with a child or children from a previous relationship. The parents may or may not have children with each other, but they come together in marriage with a desire to "blend" their two families.

These stepfamilies are formed through a number of different scenarios:

1) *A husband with children marries a wife with no children.*

Sometimes a father with children from a previous relationship will marry a woman with no children of her own. His children are either the result of a previous marriage, a cohabiting relationship or an extramarital relationship, but they are his responsibility to care for. His new bride may or may not have been married before, but she brings no children into the marriage.

2) *A wife with children marries a husband with no children.*

Sometimes the previous scenario is reversed. A wife with children from a previous relationship or marriage will marry a husband with no children of his own. He may be divorced or have never been married, but he brings no children of his own into the relationship.

3) *A divorced mom with children marries a divorced dad with kids.*

This may be the most common scenario among stepfamilies. Two previously married or cohabiting people decide to marry, and each brings a child or children from a previous relationship into the new marriage. It is the typical "Brady Bunch" scenario, where two families come together to make one large family unit. It may feel like the most fun and exciting scenario for a blended family—and it can be.

But in reality, it is likely the most challenging stepfamily situation to navigate, since there are lots of different interpersonal dynamics and temperaments involved. In some cases, it can create the "perfect storm" for conflict and friction between siblings and parents.

4) *A widow or widower with children remarries.*

Some second marriages are formed through the death of a spouse. Either the wife or husband (or both) has children from a previous marriage. Often these kinds of scenarios bring a host of unique struggles and challenges, because there is inevitably a great deal of grief and heartache involved.

The loss of a spouse or parent is devastating, and can take years to process. And people grieve in lots of different ways, providing for some special challenges for the family to bond and move forward.

5) ***Divorced or widowed parents of adult children choose to remarry.***

Often stepfamilies are formed after children have already grown and left home. These scenarios may seem like the easiest to navigate, but that's not always the case. Since the children have already left the nest, there is no daily interaction between the families, making it harder for stepchildren to bond with their new stepparent. Instead there may be feelings of jealousy and resentment. It can take years to cultivate a sense of love and intimacy within blended families, and when you don't live under the same roof, those feelings may never have time to develop unless some deliberate steps are taken.

Time to Begin

Obviously, there are other scenarios that bring stepfamilies together, but these are a few of the most common. And these are the situations we had in mind when seeking out our group of successful blended family couples to serve as our panel of experts. The couples we brought together represent a wide range of experiences and circumstances, and are made up of many different types and styles of blended families. They were as diverse as they were insightful. And the collective knowledge, wisdom and experience they share in the pages to follow are both powerful and practical. We pray that it will change your life, marriage and family for the better from this day forward.

So stay with us as we set out on this exciting journey toward the healthy—and happy—blended family you always dreamed you could have!

Section One

"Day One" Dynamics of a Blended Family

Chapter two

The Ghosts of Relationships Past

It's almost impossible to discuss the topic of blended families without dealing with the subject of divorce. And divorce is a touchy subject in any situation, especially in Christian circles.

It's true that not all blended families are products of divorce. Some are formed through the death of a spouse, or a previous extramarital relationship. Sometimes people have children out of wedlock, and other times they decide to take on the responsibility of raising children from a close relative—maybe a grandchild, or a niece or nephew. Some single people decide to adopt, and then later bring those children into a marriage. But the truth is, the majority of stepfamilies are formed through either the dissolution of a marriage, or the breakup of a long-term dating or cohabitating relationship.

Anytime a relationship dissolves, you have ghosts of the past to deal with. And these ghosts can haunt you in ways you might never have expected.

The Myth of Divorce

There is a myth about divorce that's been perpetuated by society for many years. And it's a myth that has done severe damage to the institution of marriage, as well as the stability of the family. We've been told that divorce is really not that harmful, and the affects are not necessarily long-lasting. That it's a simple solution to alleviating a bad situation. If the relationship isn't working, or begins to feel overwhelming, you fix it by putting an end to the marriage. No harm, no foul. Then you're free to try again.

We're told that children are resilient, and bounce back quickly once the breakup is over. And the lasting affects on children are not really that lasting.

We're told that divorce is inevitable when two people can't seem to get along, and that if you have to fight for your marriage, it's not worth staying together. We've trivialized the consequences of divorce, and because of it, we're often unequipped and unable to deal with the feelings of pain, remorse, and regret when they begin to haunt us—sometimes years, even decades, after the relationship has ended.

The reality is, divorce is an agonizing and brutal thing to go through, regardless of the causes behind it. Divorce is the death of a marriage relationship, and like all deaths, it leaves behind a wake of grief, pain and guilt.

Anyone who has been through a divorce knows firsthand the intense and long-term effects it can have on everyone involved—not just the husband and wife, but on the children, on their grandparents, and other extended family members and friends. The ripple effects of divorce spread far and wide, and affect far more people than just the immediate family. It is anything but harmless.

There is a reason that scripture warns believers to avoid divorce. It is God's will for marriage relationships to last a lifetime. We're even told that God "hates divorce."[1] And He expects us to honor the marriage covenant as sacred, permanent, and holy. Having said that, it's important to understand that God does not hate divorced people or those who have failed in previous relationships. In fact, the reason God hates divorce is that it harms those He loves so deeply.

If you have been through a divorce, or failed in a previous relationship, you are loved deeply by God. You might have made mistakes in the process of divorcing, or maybe you fought hard for your marriage but were abandoned, abused, or cheated on. Only God knows your specific circumstances. But you need to know that God is forgiving and gracious, and that you and your blended family are not second-class citizens. You are special to God, and His desire is to bless you, not punish you or do you harm.

The devil is so evil. He tempts us to do the wrong thing, and then when he succeeds in causing us to fall, he relentlessly condemns us for sinning. It is very common for people in blended families to live under a cloud of shame, regret, and condemnation. And those feelings are never from God. They are always lies from the devil.

God never condemns his children. When we sin, the Lord gently convicts us as He offers us grace and help in our time of need. Only the devil has an interest in focusing on our past. God wants us to be thankful for the good, forgive the bad, and learn from our mistakes. God is always for us, and never against us.

Life After Divorce

There are many views on the subject of divorce and remarriage in the body of Christ, and some teach that past divorce is a "stain" that can never be washed away. They believe that God cannot accept or forgive a divorced person, and that He refuses to bless a remarriage or a blended family. But that kind of teaching is simply not true. It's not only a misrepresentation of Scripture, but a distortion of the true nature and character of God and the power of God's forgiveness.

Above all else, God is a God of mercy, grace, and compassion. He hates divorce because of the harm it does to those He loves, but He also understands the fallen nature of man. That's what the Cross is all about. The blood that Jesus shed on the Cross was shed to cover even our greatest sins and human failings. There is no sin or offense that can keep us from the love and forgiveness of God.

Paul tells us in the book of Romans, "…all have sinned and fall short of the glory of God."[2] There's not a man or woman on earth who has not broken God's laws or commandments. We are all impure and unworthy in our own right. But through our faith in Christ, God accepts us as we are, in spite of our many flaws and shortcomings. Through Jesus we are the righteousness of God in Christ.

John tells us, "If we confess our sins, He is faithful and just and will forgive us our sins and purify us from all unrighteousness."[3]

When we come to Jesus in brokenness and repentance, all of our past sins and transgressions are forgiven. Nothing we have done in the past will be held against us. God promises to "remember our sins no more,"[4] when we come to Him and humbly ask for forgiveness. And you can always, *always* trust God's promises.

It is an insult to God's holiness to take marriage lightly. But it's also an insult to His grace and mercy to treat divorce or relationship failures as unforgivable sins.

When couples come to me (Jimmy) on the brink of divorce, my response is always to help them do whatever it takes to save the marriage. I believe in the sanctity of marriage and the power of reconciliation. I'm convinced that any marriage, no matter how broken or dysfunctional it has become, can be saved, as long as both parties are willing to try.

But there are times when reconciliation is simply not possible. Sometimes one partner is unwilling to commit to the relationship. Other times there are patterns of abuse, deceit, or sexual infidelity. Sometimes divorce is not only the most sane option, but the only safe one. There are times when an unrepentant and unfaithful spouse makes reconciliation impossible. And in those cases, it is wrong to make the innocent spouse feel judged and stigmatized.

I've counseled many couples who have remarried after a divorce, and I can tell by their countenances that most of them are embarrassed and ashamed. They know I am a pastor, and often expect me to judge them for their past divorce. They are so accustomed to feeling like second-class citizens that they just assume I will look down on them. It's always sad when people feel that way, because their fears are completely unfounded.

I teach that reconciliation is always the best approach, because I believe that in the core of my being. But once a marriage has ended and a new marriage has begun, it is wrong to dwell on the past. Because in God's economy, once we repent, our past no longer exists. God not only forgives our failings; He forgets them.

As a pastor, it's my role to help people move beyond their past, and look only to a bright future. I tell them, "I don't care if this is your second, third, or tenth marriage. I just want it to be your last marriage!" Because I truly believe that that's what God would say to them.

Walking in Forgiveness

If you have found yourself in a second or third marriage, with divorce in your past, and are still struggling to feel God's forgiveness, I encourage you to put your past behind you once and for all. Ask the Holy Spirit to reveal any hidden faults or sins you may be harboring. Things that may have played a role in the failure of your previous marriage or marriages—like pride, selfishness, anger, a critical spirit, unforgiveness, abuse, neglect, or unfaithfulness. Ask God to show you any patterns of sin and self-centeredness that still reside in your heart, and then pray for healing as you depend on God's grace for the strength to change. Come before God with open hands and a contrite heart, and be honest about your past. Then pledge to put it behind you and move forward in grace and forgiveness and a renewed vision for the future.

Maybe you haven't been divorced but have children from a previous sexual relationship. You entered into a blended marriage in hopes of putting your past behind, but now your mistakes still haunt you. You want to move forward but you struggle to believe that God has truly forgiven your past mistakes.

Regardless of your situation, ask God to forgive you, then believe that He has done just that. Trust that He has wiped your slate clean and removed your past "as far as the east is from the west."[5]

God's grace is sufficient to cover any sin or transgression you could possibly have committed. Just believe in God's power to forgive, and commit to stop walking in fear, shame, and remorse.

The Apostle Paul tells us that there is no condemnation for those who belong to Jesus.[6] Condemnation and shame are always of the devil.

There is a simple way to defeat condemnation and shame. Whenever you begin to feel guilt or remorse, begin to praise Jesus for His blood and forgiveness. The devil hates to hear about the blood of Jesus, because it defeated him two thousand years ago. And it is still defeating him today. It isn't about how good or bad we are, it is all about Jesus and His wonderful grace.

Don't let the devil trap you in a graceless past, or in a prison of condemnation and regret. Turn to Jesus and believe that He has forgiven you. And then never look back. You are God's beloved child, destined for victory.

Learning to Accept Forgiveness

Once we've learned to accept God's forgiveness and embrace His unconditional love, it's time to forgive those who have caused us pain. And this is usually easier said than done.

Many years ago, I (Frank) was involved in a business partnership that went south. The company was extremely successful, but the partnership never quite jelled. There were three of us, and we each had different personalities, and different views and opinions on the best way to grow and manage the business. We could never quite come to a consensus on important decisions. We were all young and immature at the time, and that probably added to the conflict, but we found ourselves in a constant battle of wills. We eventually decided to part ways, and since I was the junior partner, I was expected to sell my share of the company to my partners.

During the buyout negotiations, things got even more heated. I was offered far less than I thought my shares were worth, although my partners insisted that the offer was fair. The negotiations went on for many months, and no one seemed willing to budge. I eventually took the offer, just to bring closure to the deal, but I always felt that I had been cheated. Especially given the amount of time and energy I had put into helping grow the business.

I was convinced that I had put the matter behind me, but in my spirit, I still had a lot of pent-up anger and resentment.

I met my wife Ruthie just a few months after the breakup of our partnership, and we had a first date shortly afterward. I thought the date went well, but she told me later how bitter and negative I came across to her. She said I spent the entire time complaining about my former part-ners. She actually decided halfway through dinner that she didn't like me.

Thankfully, she eventually changed her mind, but it was months before she agreed to go out with me again.

The bitterness in my heart toward my former partners was affecting every area of my life. Though I had always been an optimistic person, my general attitude had slowly started to change. I'd become cynical, un-pleasant and pessimistic. I had trouble sleeping, and often found myself driving through town with the radio off, reliving many of the arguments we'd had during company meetings, thinking of all the things I "should have said to them."

I struggled to turn loose of my anger and resentment, and because of it, my entire personality had started to change. The unforgiveness in my heart and spirit was rotting my disposition from the inside out.

Learning to Forgive

That's the problem with an unforgiving spirit. It keeps us in con-stant bondage to the offense. It's like reliving a horrible experience over and over again, when we should be letting it go. Unforgiveness is like an invisible umbilical cord, keeping us attached to the offense, as well as the person who offended us. And we are constantly being fed by anger and bitterness. It continuously seeps into our system, making us sicker and weaker by the day.

Someone once said that harboring unforgiveness is like drinking poison in hopes that someone else will die from it. It's an irrational response, but a common reaction when someone has caused us pain and distress.

And there's nothing quite as painful and distressing as divorce and the breakup of an intimate relationship. Experts say that divorce can be as stressful and upsetting as the death of a child or loved one. It's one of the most agonizing events a person can go through. And it takes a willful decision to forgive in order to overcome our pain and grief.

It's almost impossible to get through a divorce without feeling an intense amount of anger and resentment—toward your ex-spouse, as well as others who may have taken their side. And those are feelings that need to be dealt with in order to truly move forward in a new blended marriage. It was years before I (Frank) was able to finally forgive my former business partners and move forward. Though our relationship was only a business arrangement, the breakup felt like a divorce to me, and I struggled deeply to get over the offense.

I still remember the day I decided to turn loose of my bitterness. I happened to run into one of my former partners while watching my four-year-old nephew play soccer. He was there with his son, and he seemed as uncomfortable with the situation as I was. It was the first time we had seen each other since the breakup of our business.

We made awkward small talk for several minutes, then suddenly he turned toward me and said, almost under his breath, "You know, we do a lot of things differently in the company these days. We're not the same people we were when you were involved. I think we've all matured quite a bit."

It wasn't a direct apology, but it did feel like something of an olive branch extended in my direction. And I decided to take it. Right then, I determined to let go of any feelings of unforgiveness I still harbored. We shook hands and went our separate ways, and I instantly felt a hundred pounds lighter. It was an immensely freeing experience for me. From that moment forward, I determined to never think poorly of them again. And I never have.

I hope they've been able to forgive me as well, because in hindsight, I was just as stubborn and unbending as they were.

If you haven't experienced that kind of freedom from resentment toward your former spouse—or anyone in your past who has done you wrong—it's time to let go. In the next few chapters, we'll discuss ways to do that, as well as some concrete steps toward seeing that any unhealthy patterns of anger and resentment don't reoccur in your present marriage.

The ghosts of relationships past can do serious harm to a blended family. So be sure you've taken steps to remove them from your heart and mind now, as you move forward in freedom and forgiveness.

Chapter
three

Four is a Crowd

My (Jimmy's) dad grew up in a blended family. His father had two children by his first wife before she died at a young age. A few years later he met a young widow who also had two children, and the two of them fell in love and got married.

Since they were both still young, they had six more children together, making it a total of ten kids in the family. I'm guessing it felt more like a zoo at times than a household, but they certainly had fun. It was one big happy family. My grandparents did a good job of successfully "blending" their two families.

Because of that, I have more cousins than I know how to count. I think it's around twenty-five on that side of the family alone. Every time we'd get together as kids it would be nothing but chaos and confusion. But it was also a lot of fun.

Some of the cousins were Evanses and the rest were Messers, from my grandmother's side, but we never knew the difference. We were just one huge tribe, all laughing and playing together in the yard, then fighting to find a place at the table so we wouldn't starve. I loved it. My grandparents proved that it's possible to successfully bring kids together in a blended family and to truly "blend." I'm sure they had their struggles along the way, but in the end, their efforts were fruitful and effective. My dad was one of the older children, and had the joy of growing up in a successful blended family.

There's no one-size-fits-all formula for successfully blending two families into one. Every situation is different, with its own unique set of challenges and struggles. My grandparents were both widowed when they met and married, so there were no past divorces to deal with. But I'm sure they still had a great deal of grief and personal loss to process.

Anytime you have a blended family, you have a history of past relationships to navigate, and all the emotional ties and baggage that goes along with it. That's true whether the children come from a previous marriage, a dating relationship, or a one-time sexual encounter.

When kids are brought into a new marriage, there is almost always some level of emotional or physical tie to a previous spouse or sexual partner. And when those feelings are unresolved, you have an unwelcome party in the relationship. When both partners bring that kind of baggage into the marriage, you have a breeding ground for trouble.

In marriage, three is a crowd. And four is a formula for disaster.

Unhealthy Emotional Ties

I (Jimmy) read once that about half of all divorced people say they still have feelings for their previous spouse ten years after the divorce. And I've seen that truth firsthand in my years as a pastor and marriage counselor.

As a teenager, I had a good friend who went on to marry his high school sweetheart. They always seemed like the perfect couple. But my friend loved to drink, and he soon developed a serious drinking problem. It quickly turned into a habit that he couldn't control. His alcoholism eventually destroyed his marriage. His wife divorced him, and he died shortly afterward.

Years later, his wife went onto marry a wonderful Christian man, who was much more stable and loving than her previous husband had been. I happened to run across them at baseball game one day and congratulated her on her new marriage. I asked her how she was doing.

"We're doing great," she said. "We're very happy." Then she paused for a second, took a step closer and added, "But I still love my first husband."

She was able to go on with her life, but her feelings for her first husband never quite went away, even after all the pain and heartache he had caused her.

It isn't easy to get over the first person you willingly let into your heart. You can move on, but often there are residual feelings lingering somewhere in your spirit.

When talking about marriage, Jesus said, "'For this reason a man will leave his father and mother and be united to his wife, and the two will become one flesh.' So they are no longer two, but one flesh."[7]

Anytime we have sexual intimacy with another person, we become one with them. We create a physical and spiritual bond with them that is profound. Society has trivialized this truth, and tried to convince us that sex is just a harmless form of fun and entertainment. But they couldn't be more wrong. Sex is a sacred and spiritual act, and it creates an intimate spiritual and emotional tie. And previous emotional ties can destroy a marriage if they aren't dealt with and effectively resolved.

Whispers of the Enemy

Karen and I (Jimmy) experienced this truth firsthand during the early years of our marriage.

When I first met Karen, we were still in high school, and I was dating another girl from our school. I was immediately smitten with Karen, so I broke up with my girlfriend in order to date her. Karen was a much better catch, and twice as pretty, so it was an easy decision on my part. But just about every time Karen and I had an argument and broke up, I'd call up my former girlfriend and ask her out. I'm still not exactly sure why I did that, but it was my natural reaction—probably as a way to get back at Karen. But also because the relationship I had with my former girlfriend was casual and sexual.

It was never long before Karen and I would make up and be back together, and I would again drop the relationship with my former girl-friend.

Karen and I were just nineteen when we married, and I was convinced I'd be the world's greatest husband. But I was far from it. I was actually an emotional bully and extremely immature, and because of it, we locked horns on a daily basis. Our first few years of marriage felt like one long argument. There were good times, to be sure, but they were far overshadowed by the bad.

During those years, every time Karen and I had a fight, I remember thinking back on my former girlfriend from high school. I'd be sitting in my Lazy Boy recliner, fuming over something Karen had said or done, and I'd think to myself, "I just married the wrong person. I should have married my other girlfriend from high school. Why did I ever leave her for Karen?"

The truth is, she and I were never that great together. We argued far more than I'd ever argued with Karen. But for some reason, my memory always seemed to be distorted and selective. All I ever remembered were the good times.

That's how Satan works to tear couples apart. Whenever he sees conflict or stress in a relationship, he capitalizes on it by whispering into our spirit, "You just married the wrong person. You'd be happier if you'd never met them. You were better off before."

He uses the memories of our past ties and relationships to destroy our present ones. And he does it because he knows it works. Satan understands the emotional ties created by previous relationships, even if we don't. And Satan will use any tool at his disposal when trying to destroy what God has joined together.

This is perhaps one of the most damaging and prevalent "day one" dynamics facing almost all blended marriages. In just about every blended family, there are remnants of past relationships, and if those memories haven't been healthily resolved, Satan will use them to tear the family apart.

Satan Slanders as We Sleep

The Apostle Paul tells us, "Do not let the sun go down while you are still angry, and do not give the devil a foothold."[8]

Another effective strategy that Satan uses to destroy families is to implant thoughts of slander and accusation. The Greek word for devil is "diabolos," which means "slanderer."

Any time we go to bed angry, we give Satan the opportunity to slander our spouse to us. He whispers false accusations into our spirit, causing us to think damaging and untrue thoughts about our spouse. I often tell people, "Every time you go to bed angry, you are being counseled by the devil, even if you don't know it." When we allow our anger to stew instead of talking things through, we give Satan a powerful foothold on our hearts and minds.

On the one hand, the devil accuses and slanders our spouse. And on the other, he brings up past relationships and selectively distorts them to where we only remember the good and forget the bad.

It was the same principle at work when the children of Israel left the bondage of Egypt with Pharoah's whips on their backs. Soon afterward, when they faced the giants in the Promised Land, they longed for their days in Egypt, completely forgetting the torture and slavery they had endured.

Satan's greatest strength is his stealth. In the Garden of Eden when the devil deceived Adam and Eve, he took the form of a serpent. Serpents are dangerous because they are stealthy and covert. They often go completely unnoticed. And that's how the devil works. He is an evil, invisible enemy that comes to us in the shadow of the night, whispering thoughts of deceit, discouragement, and offense into our minds.

In a blended family, there are going to be times when things get tough. During those moments, you have to refuse to give up, or allow the devil to build strongholds of deceit in your mind. You have to daily work through any struggle or issue that comes along, and commit to never going to bed angry.

One of the disciplines of a healthy marriage is that couples learn to work through their problems daily. They don't allow angry thoughts to grow and fester. They choose to forgive in order to keep the devil from putting his evil foot in the doorway of their minds.

Taking Thoughts Captive

If you are in a blended marriage and struggling with dangerous and selective memories of a previous relationship, it's time to take those thoughts captive and cast them from your mind. Don't let Satan use your memories to his advantage. Don't allow him to poison and distort your thoughts with lies and deceit.

There came a time in our marriage when I finally realized I needed to put my damaging memories to bed for good. The more Karen and I argued, the more I found myself dwelling on the past, fantasizing about how much better things might be if I had married my former girlfriend, instead of Karen.

Several years into our marriage, on the heels of a particularly heated argument, I remember thinking to myself, "I wonder where she is now? I wonder if she's still single? What would happen if I just walked out the door right now and left Karen for good? I'll bet we could get back together."

I know now how toxic and dangerous those thoughts were. And I realize that they were demonically inspired in order to destroy our marriage.

One of the greatest moments in our marriage came when I finally realized that the offenses I had toward Karen and the deceptive thoughts I had about my former girlfriend were happening because I was continually going to bed angry. I would lie in bed night after night with damaging thoughts swirling through my head. I would replay our arguments in my mind, and think of how bad things were with Karen, and how good they might be if I had married someone else. And then I would punish her by becoming silent for days on end, shutting her out of my heart.

The more I did that, the worse things got between us.

Then one day, while reading in the book of 2 Corinthians, the Lord revealed to me how deceived I had become. He showed me how Satan had built strongholds in my mind in order to turn my heart away from Karen. And then he showed me what I needed to do in order to overcome the devil's tactics.

Paul wrote, "For though we live in the world, we do not wage war as the world does. The weapons we fight with are not the weapons of the world. On the contrary, they have divine power to demolish strongholds. We demolish arguments and every pretension that sets itself up against the knowledge of God, and we take captive every thought to make it obedient to Christ."[9]

I realized that in order to be set free, I had to learn to take every thought captive. I had to challenge Satan's lies in order to overcome them. So I began to ask the Holy Spirit—the Spirit of Truth—to reveal to me the truth about myself, and my marriage to Karen. To help me discern lies from reality.

Slowly the scales began falling from my eyes and I could finally see things as they were. It became so clear to me how the devil had been accessing my thoughts without my knowledge. And it was my bitterness toward Karen that opened the door for him.

I immediately closed that door by forgiving Karen and asking for forgiveness—both from her and from God. It was the beginning of healing in our marriage.

I also began taking captive those damaging thoughts I had concerning my old girlfriend. Any time memories of her surfaced in my mind, I rejected the thought, and asked the Lord to break any soul ties I had with her through our sexual relations. And that was when I finally found freedom. From that point forward I never again had any serious thoughts concerning her.

The devil loves to poison our thoughts to destroy our marriages and relationships. And as he does that, he perverts our thoughts toward ex-spouses and other relationships to convince us that we made a mistake and must go back. Like the children of Israel at the border of the Promised Land, we agonize over the challenges of the present as we remember in a distorted manner the people and events of our past.

God has given us authority over the devil. But we must acknowledge that he is real. We must close the door on him and learn to take our thoughts captive. And in doing these things, we can live free in a loving and safe marriage and family.

Chapter four

Unresolved Anger and Resentment

Not all of our past memories are distorted. Sometimes the ghosts that haunt us are not untrue thoughts and memories of past relationships, but real pain and heartache that has never quite let us go.

Divorce is a horrible thing to go through. Any time a relationship ends, there is a wake of damaged feelings and emotions to deal with. And that's especially true when the relationship involved sexual intimacy. It's difficult to forgive someone who once held your heart in their hands, only to later reject you.

I see so many people go into remarriage with a chip on their shoulder. They are loaded for bear and angry at the world, and often they're the last ones to know it. They are convinced that they have put their past behind, but the feelings of anger and resentment are still there. Still simmering beneath the surface. Still seething and hurting and accusing. The wounds are still fresh, open, and untreated.

And regardless of who we're mad at, our spouse is going to take the brunt of the fury. We always take our anger out on the people closest to us. Even when they are the ones who least deserve it.

I once knew a woman who married very young and soon discovered that her new husband was a sexual predator. She caught him cheating on her a number of times, though he always denied it. When she caught him red-handed, he turned the tables and tried to blame her, claiming that she was cold and frigid in bed, causing him to look elsewhere for sex.

He would often ask her to do things in bed that felt wrong and unnatural to her, and when she refused, he would get angry and leave, usually seeking his pleasure elsewhere.

She eventually divorced him and determined to put her past behind her. A few years later she met and married a wonderful man who was nothing like her first husband. He was stable, loving, and faithful.

Still, the memories of her previous marriage lingered. She found herself constantly accusing her new husband of being unfaithful, or flirting with other women, even though he was completely innocent. She knew her suspicions were misguided and irrational, but still she struggled to overcome them.

Anytime we have unresolved anger and resentment toward another person, we risk transferring the offense onto those we love most. And this transference of guilt can happen no matter who it is we're mad at, whether it's an ex-spouse, a previous lover, a former business partner, or even a friend who wounded us. Wherever unresolved pain resides, there are defense mechanisms in place to keep us from getting hurt again.

And the only way to truly stop the cycle is to resolve the pain once and for all.

Dealing With Unresolved Anger

When we carry around unresolved pain and anger, we become like an old dog carrying around a bone. We chew on it, gnaw on it, drag it around the house, bring it to bed with us, even curl up with it as we sleep. We become dependent on it, and find a strange kind of security in knowing it is near. When someone tries to take it away, we growl and snap at them. We protect our pain like it is some kind of needed treasure.

We hang onto our pain because it brings us comfort. But all it is doing is keeping us from grabbing hold of things that are much more healthy and rewarding. And the only real solution to being free is to bury it deep in the ground and leave it there—never to dig it up again.

There are simple and powerful steps you can take to completely forgive the people who have wounded and offended you, and to be set free from hurt, bitterness, and unforgiveness. These steps can help you overcome the pain from prior abuse, abandonment, betrayal, rejection, and suffering. As you follow these directives, you are cutting the umbilical cord that connects you to the people and pain of your past. You are also closing the door on the devil and his foothold into your heart, and opening the door for God to move in and heal you.

Here are four simple steps to truly forgiving those who have hurt us:

1) *Realize that unforgiveness is a sin.*

In the book of Matthew, Jesus teaches us how to pray by reciting what you and I have come to know as the Lord's Prayer. It is a daily prayer, and includes a confession to God.

"Forgive us our debts as we forgive our debtors."[10]

After reciting the prayer, Jesus reiterates the importance of this teaching by saying, "For if you forgive other people when they sin against you, your heavenly Father will also forgive you. But if you do not forgive others their sins, your Father will not forgive your sins."[11]

According to Jesus, forgiving others is a condition of being forgiven. Unforgiveness isn't just a problem—it is a sin. It is refusing to extend to others the same grace that God has extended to us. We all want grace from God for ourselves, but when it comes to those who have offended us, we prefer justice.

In Luke chapter six, Jesus reminds us that if we are merciful, we will receive mercy from God. If we do not judge others we will not be judged. But forgiveness is conditional. God will give us as much grace as we choose to give others. It is that simple.

I'm in need of a lot of grace from God, and I'm sure you are, too. But in order to receive that grace, we have to be willing to extend it to others. If you are harboring bitterness and unforgiveness from the past, freedom begins when you confess that sin to God and ask for His forgiveness.

The good news is, He always responds. He generously forgives, because it is in His gracious nature to do so.

2) Disqualify yourself as their judge.

My (Jimmy's) dad wasn't a good father while I was growing up. He was a workaholic, emotionally detached, unaffectionate, and never a big part of my life. The older I got the angrier I became toward him. I just couldn't understand how he could be so distant and unavailable. Then one day my aunts told me a story about his childhood that I had never heard. They told me about the abject poverty he had grown up in during the Great Depression. As a young boy, he had to sleep outside on a cot every night, and in the winter he would sleep with the horses in order to stay warm. He only ate meat once a week because his parents had so little money for food. He didn't even have a pair of shoes, and it deeply shamed him.

I had never known those things about my father, and when my aunts shared that with me, I suddenly saw my father in a different light. I understood his pain, and that allowed me to give him grace. I no longer resented him for the way he treated me as a child. I instead felt tremendous love and compassion.

When we understand why people do the things they do, it brings a level of insight and grace into our hearts. We realize how wrong it is to judge them for their actions. God is the only one who can judge, because He is the only one who sees the scars and demons from our past.

True forgiveness begins by acknowledging our limited perspective of others, and relinquishing the temptation to judge. We trust God to be both judge and jury. And we give up our right to seek vengeance. If there are legal matters that need to be dealt with, we commit to doing so with a right spirit.

3) Give your offender a high value.

You and I have a natural tendency to harbor unforgiveness and judgment toward others. And we do that by devaluing them as a person. We assign labels, like "idiot," "jerk," "witch," "loser," or "moron." Because through labeling them, we devalue their worth, and give ourselves permission to harbor feelings of ill will.

But God loves all of us the same, even those who have hurt us. Regardless how much abuse or shame they have caused us, He still loves and values them. He may not approve of their behavior, but He understands their pain, and He chooses to extend grace.

For true forgiveness to occur, we must remove judgments and labels and admit that God loves those who have offended us, even if they are unbelievers. God created them in their mother's wombs, and He loves them deeply. To walk in true grace and forgiveness, we must learn to see people through God's eyes. The more we do, the easier it will be to forgive others and give them grace.

4) Pray for your offender.

Jesus said to His followers, "But to you who are listening I say: Love your enemies, do good to those who hate you, bless those who curse you, pray for those who mistreat you … Do to others as you would have them do to you."[12]

This may be one of the most challenging commandments Jesus ever gave us, but He did so for a reason. It's virtually impossible to hold a grudge against someone you are actively praying for over a period of time. It's also hard to stay offended at a person when your mouth is speaking blessings over them. Jesus' commandment isn't just trite spiritual advice. It is the most important thing we do in the process of forgiveness to heal our wounded hearts.

As I've counseled people over the years, I can't count the number of times people have said to me, "Jimmy, I keep trying to forgive them, but regardless of how many times I pray, I still feel the same bitterness and hurt towards them." I completely understand their dilemma, because I have experienced the same thing many times.

I can only think of two people in my life that I have truly hated. Both of them did things to me and my family that were unthinkable. I found myself despising them, and eventually, my contempt began to change my personality for the worse. More than that, it began to negatively affect my marriage. I found myself acting out in ways that were completely irrational, because my heart was filled with such hatred and disdain.

Then one day, while reading in the book of Luke, God began to convict me to pray for the man that I hated so much. Jesus said, "But to you who are listening I say: Love your enemies, do good to those who hate you, bless those who curse you, pray for those who mistreat you."[13]

The thought of praying for the man who had done me wrong was extremely distasteful to me. But the Lord was unrelenting, and I knew that bitterness was consuming my heart. So I began praying daily for both of these people. It wasn't easy, but I was committed to obeying Jesus' command.

Within a couple of weeks, my attitude toward them changed. I found myself absent of bitterness and negative feelings. As I was praying for them, God was lancing my heart and draining away the infection.

And something else happened. In place of the pain, I began to feel peace, even compassion. My obedience to Jesus' command was the final step in allowing my heart to be totally healed, and for the pain of my past to be resolved.

If you can relate to this story, I encourage you to do the same. Begin today praying for those who have hurt you, and asking God to bless them. Whether they are still in your life, or far away in your past, commit to keeping them in your prayers daily. As you take the steps to obey Jesus, you are walking into your healing, and into God's best for your family and future.

Taking the First Step

There are many dynamics involved in healthily resolving damaging pain and issues from the past. In some cases, it takes counseling from a qualified professional to effectively work through the process. There are some issues that are simply too complex and complicated to process on our own, and the best thing we can do is to admit we need help, and then actively seek it out.

Growing a healthy blended marriage is worth any amount of work you have to put into it. So we encourage you to do all you can to resolve any harmful and damaging emotions now, before it is too late.

A journey of a thousand miles begins with the first step, and the same is true with any process of healing. Whether you are dealing with false memories of your past relationships, unresolved anger and resentment, or any other ghosts from the past that haunt you, healing begins the moment you decide to stand up and start to walk.

Begin your journey today.

chapter five

Lowered Trust & Higher Expectations

There's a reason that cars come with front windshields that are four feet wide and two feet high, but rearview mirrors that are only about eight inches long. When driving, you're supposed to keep your eyes focused forward. It's the only safe way to travel. You have to know where you're going, and then fix your eyes firmly on the road ahead so you can get there safely.

Imagine if we tried to drive a car with our eyes fixed on the rearview mirror. What would happen if we were so focused on where we'd been that we completely forgot to look where we are going?

You know the answer. We wouldn't get fifty feet without hurting someone, or causing all sorts of chaos and confusion. There's no telling what damage we might do, or how many head-on collisions we would cause. The road around us could be strewn with crashed cars and wounded pedestrians, and we wouldn't even know it, because we'd be too fixated on the past to see the mayhem we were causing.

We'd never get very far, and we certainly wouldn't get where we wanted to go.

Sadly, that's how a lot of people approach their remarriages. They get behind the wheel intending to look forward to a bright and promising future. But they soon find themselves fixated on the rearview mirror. They come into the marriage with so much pain and bitterness that they're afraid to look forward. Their mind is so obsessed with where they've been that they completely forget to focus on where they want to go.

As a result, they leave a wake of confusion and destruction in their path. And they seldom even see the damage they are causing to those around them. Their path is strewn with wounded hearts, battered egos, and bloodied self-images, but they seem completely oblivious to the chaos they are creating.

A Dangerous Combination

In almost every remarriage there are two very real dynamics that couples have to overcome. They are two of the most damaging "day one" dynamics a remarried couple has to navigate, and they are as common as they are detrimental. And I (Jimmy) see them at work just about every time a newly remarried couple comes to me for counseling.

The first is a lowered level of trust. People who have been through a divorce on the heels of a bad marriage are normally going to feel less trustful when it comes to relationships. They've been wounded before, and they don't want to be wounded again. Often they've been deceived, betrayed, and mistreated. They've felt the sting of rejection. They've willingly given their heart to another, only to have it broken and handed back to them. They struggle to trust because they've done that before, only to have their trust violated.

The second is a higher level of expectation. People who have been hurt in the past tend to be more cynical, sensitive, and suspicious. They are not willing to be as patient and long-suffering as they once were. Their last partner failed to live up to their expectations, and somewhere deep in their spirit they expect their new partner to fail them as well. So they closely monitor every word and action, and tend to be constantly on their guard.

Lowered trust and higher expectations is the ultimate "one-two" combination. It's not only unfair; it creates a standard that's virtually impossible to attain, and can easily implode a marriage.

Lowered Trust

In most first marriages, couples come into the marriage with lots of hope and optimism in their new relationship. Often they've been dating for a while, and are driven by infatuation. While dating, couples always put their best foot forward. They are so in love that they can't imagine ever being disappointed. So they give their heart willingly, trusting that it will be well tended.

And when relationships go bad, trust is often the first thing to go.

Trust is not just important to couples. It is central to the success of any marriage relationship. Without it, no relationship can survive for the long haul.

According to Dr. John Gottman, when social psychologists ask single people, "What is the most desirable quality you're looking for in a dating partner?" the number one answer is "trustworthiness."[14]

Trust is far more than an added benefit to a healthy relationship. It is an essential requirement. It is one of the foundational attributes of any successful marriage.

And trustworthiness means more than just being sexually faithful. In marriage, trust involves a wide range of needs and emotions.

We trust our partner to be emotionally faithful. Wives need their husbands to love and cherish them—and them alone—and husbands need their wives to honor and respect them above all others. Couples need to know that they can trust each other to stay true to the marriage covenant, both physically and emotionally.

We trust our partner not to harm or reject us. Marriage relationships have to feel completely safe and secure, and free of verbal or physical abuse. When one partner tries to control the other, or when we treat each other with dishonor and disrespect, it rips the very fabric of the trust relationship.

We trust each other to love without condition or stipulation, regardless of the circumstances. When we recite our wedding vows, we pledge to stay faithful in sickness and health, through good and bad times, for richer or poorer, until death parts us. And we need to know that we can trust each other to uphold those vows.

We trust that our partner won't abandon us in the midst of conflict or disagreement. We need to know that the marriage is more important than any argument or struggle that comes against it, and that our partner is just as committed to getting through tough times as we are.

We trust each other to put the marriage first, in all situations. That our partner will love, honor, and cherish us no matter what happens. That the marriage is always the top priority, no matter what other needs or activities clamor for our attention. That we will never be taken for granted, or neglected, or lost in the shuffle.

We promise to give the best we have to offer to the sanctity of marriage, and we trust our partner to do the same. And when that trust becomes broken or violated, it creates a deep violation in the marriage relationship.Anytime a marriage fails, there has been an undeniable breach of trust. There are very real wounds that take time and attention to be healed.
There are offenses that are deep and can only be resolved by faith in God and true forgiveness. And there is violated trust that is real and undeniable, and can only be resolved by an act of the will and the grace of God.

It's not surprising that almost all blended marriages struggle with issues of lowered trust. Once you've been burned deeply, the scars and the pain are reminders of the trust you gave away innocently—maybe even naively—and now you regret your decision, and don't want to experience it again.

Higher Expectations

In first marriages, people are almost always innocent until proven guilty, but the second time around, we're not so quick to extend grace. This time, spouses often become guilty until proven innocent.

It's not fair, but it's a natural response. Once we've been burned, our expectations tend to be higher, and often much more unrealistic.

A man who watched his first marriage implode because of his wife's infidelity will naturally struggle with trust issues. When he remarries, he will likely be instinctively suspicious, even if his new wife is nothing like his former one. He may call her phone several times during the day, just to see what she is doing. He may monitor her texts and emails when she isn't looking, and get suddenly angry anytime he sees her talking to another man. He will hold her to a higher standard of accountability, even if she has done nothing to warrant it.

A woman who had been previously married to a man who was cold and uncaring, who spent too much time at work, and who made her feel lonely and unwanted, will tend to be hypersensitive to these types of behavior. She may remarry a caring and attentive man, but still struggle to feel secure. She accuses him of being distant and aloof, even when he comes home on time each day to spend time with the family. She may expect him to anticipate her needs, even before she articulates them. She remembers what it feels like to be ignored and unappreciated, and she's intent on not letting it happen again. So she holds him to an unrealistic standard of attention.

We are all born with natural defense mechanisms, and the more we are hurt, the more instinctive our defenses become. We are not as quick to forgive, not as likely to be blindsided, not as willing to extend trust, not as apt to leave ourselves as open and vulnerable as we once were.

"Stands With a Fist"

In the movie "Dances With Wolves," Kevin Costner played the role of John Dunbar, a white man who fell in love with a woman who had been raised by Indians. The Indians had named the young woman "Stands With a Fist," and in one scene, Dunbar asked her how she came to get that name.

She told him that when she first came to live with the Indians, there was a woman who didn't like her. Every day this woman would taunt her and call her names. Until one day the woman went too far, so she doubled up her fist and knocked the woman to the ground.

"I was not very big, but she fell down," the girl told him. "She fell hard and didn't move. I stood over her with my fist and asked if any other woman wanted to call me bad names … No one bothered me after that day."

"I wouldn't think so," said John Dunbar. I've known some remarried people who could be given that same name. In every situation they "Stand With a Fist," just waiting to be challenged. They know what it's like to have their patience tested. They've been picked on and disrespected. They've been made to feel small and insignificant. They've had their feelings hurt once too often, and they're not willing to take it anymore. So they stand with their fists clenched tightly, saying, "Who else is going to hurt me? Who else wants to call me bad names?"

Even if their new partner is completely innocent, they still bear the brunt of their wrath. The problem is, no marriage can survive that level of mistrust and misplaced anger. It's wrong to have unrealistic and unwarranted expectations. It's not fair to hold a new spouse accountable for the sins of an old one.

No marriage can move forward when one partner is constantly looking in the rearview mirror. Continually focused on the past. Repeatedly fixing their gaze on where they've been, instead of focusing on where they need to go. That's one of the reasons the divorce rate is higher among second and third marriages. People who have been wounded in the past often expect more from the marriage than their partner is able to give them. They have less trust, and higher expectations. And that's a deadly combination to bring into a relationship.

For a blended family to work, it's critical that everyone involved commits to staying in the moment. You have to determine to let the past go and look only to the future. You can't build a meaningful relationship with someone when you are constantly on your guard, vigilantly guarding your marriage from the ghosts of the past.

Marriage relationships have to be built on mutual trust and realistic expectations; otherwise they are headed for trouble.

Steps to Rebuilding Trust

If you have found yourself struggling with these types of trust issues in your marriage, it's time to stop looking back and start focusing on what's ahead. Your family deserves the best you have to offer, and often that takes an intentional level of effort and determination. Trust issues take humility, honesty, and work to overcome, but it's something you have to do in order to build a healthy blended family.

Any time couples come to me with trust issues in their marriage, I encourage them to begin implementing three simple, but effective steps to reestablishing trust and realigning marital expectations.

First, begin to date again and keep the romance alive.

In first marriages, it's easy for couples to continue dating after the wedding, because there are no children involved, and life is pretty simple. Dating is second nature to them, since they've been dating for many months already. They don't have to be reminded, because the romance is still fresh and new.

But too often that's not the case in blended marriages. From day one, there are children to deal with, and numerous financial obligations to meet. The relationship tends to take a back seat to parenting and bills and other household responsibilities. So dating can quickly become a thing of the past.

But dating is a way to establish trust and communication. It's the one time during the week where couples can just focus on each other, instead of the demands of raising a family. Through dating, you learn about your partner's dreams, desires and ambitions. You reestablish lost feelings of romance and attraction. You are able to connect with each other, just one on one, with no bills or kids or housework there to distract you.

Through dating, you're reminded why you fell in love in the first place. And you have the opportunity to fall in love all over again, each time you go out.

If you haven't been dating your spouse, then begin to reestablish that habit this week. Your marriage must come first, and you must have quality and quantity time alone in order to connect and to establish a foundation of trust.

Second, learn to disassociate the past from the present.

Your present spouse is not responsible for the sins of your previous one, so it's time to stop transferring the blame. Any time you find yourself angry with your spouse, stop and ask yourself, "Is this a legitimate complaint? Or am I really just angry at someone else?"

So often our frustrations are misplaced and misapplied. We may find ourselves picking a fight with our spouse, when we're really just angry with our ex, or our stepchild, or the clerk at the grocery store that took her sweet time ringing us up.

Anytime we are tired and frustrated, we tend to take it out on the one closest to us. And the first step to reversing that unfair habit is to begin taking control of our emotions. We have to learn to bite our tongue when we feel like lashing out, and instead process our thoughts before speaking.

The Apostle James tells us, "Everyone should be quick to listen, slow to speak and slow to become angry, because human anger does not produce the righteousness that God desires."[15]

If we find ourselves constantly lashing out and criticizing those closest to us, the problem usually lies within our own angry spirit, not their behavior. We have to learn to step back and take a good hard look at the situation—not from our point of view, but theirs. Who are we really mad at? What is the true source of our anger and frustration?

If we find that we've been transferring blame onto our partner from past wounds and injustices, it's important to start dealing with our anger and start moving forward, instead of dwelling on the past.

Third, dream new dreams together.

The prophet Amos asked the question, "Can two walk together, unless they are agreed?"[16] The obvious answer is, "no." It's impossible to walk with someone unless you are going the same direction. You have to be going to the same place, and at the same pace.

Too often, married couples try to walk together when they are headed in different directions. They have different views on where the family should be going, and how to get there. They have different dreams and visions for the future, and they've never taken the time to compare notes and dream those dreams together.

Marriage only works when couples have a shared vision for the future, and a well-conceived plan to get there.

One of the best things you can do for your marriage—and your family—is to spend time talking about your goals and ambitions for the future. Talk about where you want to be five, ten, twenty, and fifty years from now. Discuss your hopes and dreams for your children, your finances, your career, your home, and anything else that pertains to your family.

Dream these dreams together, then put in place a solid plan of action to help you get where you both want to go.

I encourage couples to take a "Vision Retreat" at least once a year. Karen and I (Jimmy) have done that for many years and it has done more to strengthen our marriage and family than anything else. Once a year we go away to a secluded place and spend three or four days discussing every aspect of our lives. We talk about our relationship, kids and grandkids, the direction of our ministry, the state of our home and finances, and our budget for the coming year. Nothing is off the table for discussion. We use the time to assess the past year, and reestablish goals for the coming year, just to make sure we stay on track and on the same page. And we write everything down so we can remember it and stay accountable to it. We have done this for over twenty-five years and it is a transforming discipline.

When you take your first vision retreat, you may have some conflict. You may discover that you don't see eye-to-eye on some issues, and have differing visions for your future. This may cause frustration and division between you. But don't give up. Make a commitment before you go that you are going to pray and talk until you believe you know God's will for every area of your life and marriage. The most important step in the process is to submit your marriage and family to God. That way it isn't two stubborn wills colliding—it is two submitted hearts seeking to become one under God.

If you haven't done that with your spouse, I encourage you to start this year. There is no greater way to establish trust and build healthy expectations than to spend quality time together, and come to a mutual agreement regarding your shared vision for your marriage and family.

If you've never had a vision retreat with your spouse, I encourage you to visit our website and get copy of my book, *The Mountaintop of Marriage*. This resource outlines everything you need to know about having a productive and helpful vision retreat. You can find it at www.marriagetoday.com.

Looking to the Future

A few years ago, actor Tom Hanks played the lead character in a movie called "Larry Crowne." In the film, Larry was a likeable middle-aged man who was struggling to overcome a series of bad events. His marriage had ended, and soon afterward he lost his job in a retail store, making it impossible to afford his car and house payment. He enrolled in community college in order to better himself.

In one poignant scene, we see him pulling away from his house after losing it to foreclosure. His SUV is filled with his belongings, and as he drives away, his eyes are fixed on the car's rearview mirror. He tries to look forward, but can't bear to stop looking back at the home he is leaving behind. You can feel his pain as he fights back tears of regret and grief. He is leaving behind years of uncomfortable memories and disappointments. You can see the pain in his face as he steadily drives away.

Then slowly, he starts to look at the road ahead, and his car picks up the pace. Little by little, he begins to inch his eyes away from the rearview mirror. He longs for a future brighter than his past, so he painstakingly forces himself to look away. Gradually we see his eyes shift away from the rearview mirror and focus instead on the road ahead. His car picks up speed as he turns the corner ahead, leaving his old life behind.

It's a powerful scene, and anyone who has had unwanted and unwelcome change come into their lives can relate. Life doesn't always happen the way we envision. Sometimes bad things happen, and they just keep happening, until one day you wake up and nothing in your world feels familiar to you. People don't always live up to their promises. Jobs don't always pan out the way you'd hoped. Sometimes marriages don't work out, and suddenly your whole world is turned upside down.

When that happens, the only healthy approach is to find a way to put the past behind and move forward. You have to tear your eyes away from the rearview mirror and instead focus on the road ahead. The windshield in front of you is the only safe place to fix your gaze.

Don't let yourself be immobilized by pain and regret. Put it behind you once and for all, and trust God to lead you into a bright and promising future.

Chapter

Unhealthy Inner Vows

I (Jimmy) have a friend who was never allowed to have soft drinks as a boy. His mother wouldn't allow them in the house. When he told me that, I thought it was funny. But he thought it was child abuse.

He told me that one day he got so frustrated with his mother's rule that he stood in the middle of his parents' kitchen and said to her, "When I grow up I'm going to have a Coke machine right in the middle of my living room, and anyone who wants one can have them for free!"

When Karen and I started attending Trinity Fellowship in Amarillo, he and his wife were one of the first couples we met, and we became good friends. One day they invited us to their house for dinner, and as soon as we walked in the door he offered us a soft drink. He had every brand you could imagine. When I saw his pantry I couldn't believe my eyes. It looked like the soft drink aisle of a grocery store. He had more soft drinks than I had ever seen in any person's home.

His wife once told me what it was like to go grocery shopping with him. She said that when they get to the soft drink aisle he starts loading the cart with them. One time he was loading the cart with two-liter bottles of soft drinks, and she asked him, "Do we really need all these drinks?"

He instinctively snapped at her and said, "Don't tell me how much I can buy! I'm going to get all the drinks I want! Don't tell me I can't get them!"

He actually started an argument right there in the middle of the grocery store. She said she learned not to ask about it anymore, since it seemed like such a sore spot with him.

Quite honestly, I thought my friend's obsession with soft drinks was a little bit "crazy," and when I heard the story of his childhood, I understood why. Because of his mother's insistence that he not drink cokes as a child, he developed an unusual fixation on carbonated beverages. He had been denied something he wanted, and it caused him to make an irrational inner vow. He couldn't wait to grow up and get a place of his own, so he could buy all the drinks he wanted.

The inner vow he made as a child became a guiding preoccupation within him as an adult. He became obsessed with soft drinks, and the thought of running out of them became a source of great anxiety.

Defining Inner Vows

Inner vows are promises we make to ourselves in times of difficulty, turmoil, or pain. And they can easily become the force that guides our lives and actions when we become adults. Any area in which we feel betrayed, mistreated, or powerless creates within us the potential for a dangerous and unhealthy inner vow. And wherever we have an inner vow, we become irrational and un-teachable. Our actions may feel perfectly reasonable, but they don't make sense to anyone but us. To others they seem illogical, and even a bit crazy.

In my friend's case, he was denied the pleasure of drinking soft drinks as a child, and it somehow felt completely unfair to him. Every time he watched one of his friends drinking a Coke or a Dr. Pepper, it reminded him again how unjust and random his mother's rules seemed to be. And he became obsessed with the idea of drinking all the soft drinks he wanted. So much so, that even as an adult, his preoccupation with carbonated beverages stayed with him. More than that, it grew even worse.

Inner vows take on many different shapes and forms, and not all are quite so glaring, or easy to recognize. Some are more subtle, while others are far more damaging and unhealthy.

And we all have them. I've never known a person to reach adulthood without having some form of inner vow somewhere within them. We've all been wounded, and we've all felt the sting of rejection, abuse, or neglect—though obviously to varying degrees. And because of it, we've all made promises to ourselves in order to keep from getting hurt again.

A young girl who grows up with a cold and distant mother will likely be left longing for affection. She snuggles next to her mother in bed, only to feel her tense up and pull away. In her heart, the young girl craves the warmth and attention she doesn't get, so she says to herself, "I'll never treat my children that way when I have kids. I'm going to be affectionate and loving."

The young girl grows up to have children of her own, and she begins smothering them with affection. She may even develop an unnatural need to be close to her kids at all times. People see her as a doting young mother, but in reality, she is simply reacting to an unhealthy inner vow she made as a child. In doing so, she runs the risk of alienating her children because of her own exaggerated need for physical and emotional affection.

A young boy in grade school may find himself the target of bullies twice his size. Every day they pick on him, and he feels powerless to stop it. Then one day he decides he's had enough, and he fights back. He gets the brunt of the beating, but still, the satisfaction of hitting back feels good to him. As he stands in front of the mirror, wiping the blood from his nose, he says to himself, "I'm never going to let anyone pick on me again! I'm never going to take that kind of abuse!"

When the boy gets older, he starts working out in the gym every day after school, determined to bulk up. Soon he is bigger and stronger than all of his friends, yet still he continues lifting weights in an effort to get even larger.

He may even become a bully himself in order to let others know that he's not afraid of getting hurt. On the surface, he appears to be just another testosterone-filled high school kid, but in reality, he is acting out an unhealthy inner vow he made as a child. He is intent on never again being victimized by bullies. And because of it, he allows himself to become the very thing he hates the most.

My Greatest Fear

Inner vows are seldom rational, and almost always have the reverse effect that we think they will. They are intended to protect us from harm, but they almost always create even more chaos and pain. We make them innocently in order to keep us from going back to the place of pain again. But in reality, inner vows guarantee that we will do just that.

As a young boy, I (Frank) grew up feeling extremely poor. We lived in a very modest house, with seven of us sharing one tiny bathroom. My father was a disabled veteran, so we lived on a very small fixed income. And I always felt guilty when I had to ask for clothes or basic school supplies that I needed. I knew my parents were struggling to get by, and I never wanted to be a burden to them.

I remember one Saturday morning sitting in my parents' bedroom, watching my mom iron and fold huge piles of fresh, white laundry. She had been hired by a local hotel to clean and launder their dirty linens. Every morning she would drive to the hotel to pick up another carload of dirty laundry, and then spend the day washing, ironing, and folding enormous piles of white linen. She was excited about the job because the manager allowed her to do the work at home, instead of having to spend all day at the hotel.

I asked how much she made, and she explained that they paid her a flat rate of twenty-five cents per sheet. For towels, she was paid a nickel each, and pillowcases were four for a dime.

She and I talked for hours that day in the bedroom as she slaved away, processing enormous piles of laundry. I don't remember how long she worked, only that it took her the better part of the day. When she finished, she sat at the kitchen table, adding up her total pay for the day. She had made just over fifteen dollars.

She seemed pleased by the amount, but I remember thinking how little that was for an entire day of work. I had always felt poor, but never quite as much as I did at that moment.

My dad wasn't allowed to work because of his disability, but he was constantly on the lookout for ways to make extra money. He took on five paper routes with the local newspaper, and spent every weekend doing odd jobs around town, whether it was uprooting tree stumps, cleaning out vacant homes, or mowing empty lots for a local realtor.

My parents were the hardest working people I knew, yet they had very little to show for it.

I have a vivid memory of lying awake in my bed one night as a child, thinking about how much stress my parents were under as they struggled to pay the bills each month. And I thought to myself, "I'm never going to allow myself to be that poor when I grow up. I don't ever want to live with that kind of worry!"

That moment marked the beginning of a very unhealthy inner vow that I still struggle with to this day. For as long as I can remember, the thought of being poor has always been my biggest fear.

I began working at the age of twelve, selling newspapers on the corner of a busy intersection. Every afternoon after school I would gather up the leftover papers from my father's routes, and run to the corner of North Third and Sayles Blvd., just three blocks from our home, and sell papers to passing motorists during the evening rush hour. I had a number of regular customers who drove by every day to buy a paper from me. And since I was a young boy, they would always tip well.

At fifteen I went to work in a bakery washing dishes, and six years later I was working there full time, frying donuts and baking pies. I was going to school and working forty to fifty hours a week. My grades in high school suffered because of my long hours, but work was more important than school to me. Each year during summer break I would take on a second job, and then on the weekends, I would mow neighborhood lawns for extra money. I became obsessed with making money.

While my friends were having fun playing and enjoying their summer breaks, I would be working around the clock, always looking for ways to earn even more.

My friends assumed that I was an over-ambitious workaholic, but that was never true. I was simply driven by an unhealthy fear of being poor. The inner vow I made as a child became the guiding force of my life. I've committed to overcome this irrational fear, and today, I believe I've developed a healthy balance.

A Need to Control

I (Jimmy) came into adulthood with a number of deeply destructive inner vows. As a young boy I felt abused and betrayed by people who had authority over me, and I was powerless to do anything about it.

I grew up in Amarillo, Texas, and during those years, the school boards had a bad habit of redrawing school lines every few years. As a result, I was forced several times during my childhood to change school districts. Each time that happened, I'd have to leave my friends behind and go to a different school. It always felt completely unfair to me. I couldn't understand why I was being punished by people I had never even met. And for no apparent reason. I began to act out and rebel in ways that I never had before.

This happened to me several times during my childhood, and again during my middle school years. Each time, it felt even more random and unfair. I became deeply angry and offended at everyone involved with the school. One day I was so enraged by the unfairness that I vowed I would never again allow myself to be taken advantage of. I was intent on getting back at anyone who had ever wronged me, and on never letting it happen again.

As a result, I turned into one of the most unruly kids in school. I was a large kid, and already intimidating to many of those around me, but I became an even bigger terror. I was committed to never again being abused or put down by others. I took that attitude into marriage, and because of it, I was a horrible husband to Karen. I refused to admit when

I was wrong, and quickly became an emotional bully. I was stubborn, obstinate, and angry. And I had to get the upper hand in every argument, no matter how small or insignificant the matter might have been.

The inner vows I made as a young boy caused me to act out in ways that were neither sane nor rational, yet they were the only ways I knew to process the pain I had experienced at the hands of those who had done me wrong. I was unequipped to deal with the inner wounds in my spirit, so I acted out in the only way I knew how. I became a dominating husband and an emotional bully.

My attitude very nearly destroyed our marriage, and I thank God every day for stepping in and saving us from an almost certain divorce. At a point in our marriage when I had done almost irreparable harm, God brought conviction to my heart and spirit to deal with my inner pain before it completely shattered our marriage for good.

We All Have Them

In my many years as a pastor and marriage counselor, I've counseled many people on the heels of divorce, or a failed relationship, and I've yet to run across one who wasn't struggling with deep seated feelings of pain and resentment. It's very difficult to get through the breakdown of a relationship without feeling a great deal of anger, remorse, and bitterness. And wherever those types of feelings reside, you almost certainly have damaging inner vows to deal with.

"I'll never let anyone treat me like that again!"

"No one will ever speak to my kids that way again!"

"I'll never allow anyone to cheat on me, or lie to my face the way he did!"

On the heels of pain and heartache, these dangerous inner vows set up shop in our hearts and falsely promise to guard our hearts from ever getting hurt again. They become the defense mechanisms we instinctively turn to in order to survive.

But they also become one of the greatest hurdles we have to building intimacy within marriage. In a blended family, inner vows must be recognized and broken in order to experience true happiness and intimacy.

Of all the "day one" dynamics that blended families have to deal with, this is one of the most common—and destructive— I've witnessed. Damaging inner vows are almost universal among those who have been through the breakup of a relationship, and they can cause more conflict among remarried couples than perhaps any other dynamic.

And when children are involved, they are almost certainly struggling with many hurtful inner vows of their own. Children who have experienced the divorce or separation of their parents are inevitably suffering through difficult issues of anger, abandonment, or powerlessness. They are likely dealing with deep-seated feelings of resentment and confusion, even if they don't initially show it.

Wherever pain is present, inner vows are certain to be there, usually hidden somewhere deep beneath the surface.

Overcoming Inner Vows

The worst thing you can do with inner vows is to try to ignore them. The most naïve approach you can take is to pretend that they aren't there, assume that they will somehow work themselves out in time, or believe that they will go away on their own—because they won't. Inner vows have to be dealt with before they can be truly overcome.

The good news is that inner vows can be easily broken and overcome. Here are three important steps to help recognize and break inner vows.

1. Understand why inner vows are wrong.

In reading about inner vows someone might say, "I understand that

I may have made a vow in my past but I don't see why it is so wrong." Jesus told us in Matthew chapter five that we are not to swear by heaven or earth, but to instead perform our oaths to the Lord.

The reason inner vows are wrong is because they are vows we make to ourselves, and in any area where we have made a self-promise, we are the lords of that area, not Jesus.

When you make yourself a promise like, "I'll never be poor again," then who becomes lord over your finances?

When you vow to yourself, "No one is ever going to hurt me again," then who becomes lord of your relationships? It isn't Jesus. It is you.

Inner vows are self-made, self-directed and self-protected. And the key word is "self." When we are in pain we should give it to Jesus and ask Him to heal, guide, and guard us. But inner vows do the opposite. We turn inward, and comfort ourselves with self-vows rather than turning to God.

Inner vows may feel innocent and normal, but they are sinful, because they make us god of any area of our lives where a vow is operating.

2. Identify and renounce the vow(s).

Whenever I (Jimmy) teach on the topic of inner vows, most people can immediately identify one or more vows they have made in the past. It isn't that difficult to see. But in some cases it takes more time. In dealing with inner vows, it's important to pray and ask the Holy Spirit to reveal to us any inner vows we may have made in the past—things we may have forgotten.

Any area of our lives in which we become defensive, unapproachable, un-teachable, or fearful is likely under the influence of an inner vow. These are all signs of previous pain, and a strong indication that some kind of self-oriented promise is present and needs to be broken.

Once you recognize that you have an inner vow, the first step in overcoming it is to go before God in prayer, saying, "Lord Jesus, I realize I have sinned by making a vow to myself. I didn't realize it was wrong. It was simply an attempt to ease the pain and bring comfort. I now realize that I made myself lord of that area of my life rather than turning to You. I renounce my vow and break it. I ask You to forgive me. And I receive your forgiveness. I break the power of this vow, and all of its influence over my life, in Jesus' Name."

3. Submit the area to God, and open yourself to the input of others.

The final step in breaking inner vows is to submit to God and humble yourself to others. When we are operating under the influence of a vow, we become un-teachable and irrational, even though our actions may feel sane and reasonable. We have likely established patterns of thinking and behavior that need to be broken.

And the first step toward change is to submit to the Lordship of Jesus. This means praying before making any decisions, and consulting the Bible in order to discern truth from falsehood. For instance, someone who vowed to themselves that they would never again allow themselves to be poor needs to submit their finances to God in order to break that vow. Before making any financial decisions, they should consult scripture, and pray for God's guidance and direction.

It's also important to become humble and teachable, and to begin seeking input from those we trust. Because inner vows cause us to be overly sensitive and defensive, we have to train ourselves to accept the advice and influence of others. Inner vows are created through a lack of trust, so teaching ourselves to trust again is an important step in overcoming them. If your inner vows have strained your relationship with your spouse, you should go to them and say, "Honey, I realize that I have an inner vow from my past that has been affecting our relationship. I didn't realize it was there, but now that I'm aware of it, I have committed to breaking it and submitting that area of my life to Jesus. I also want you to know that I am very sorry for how this has affected and hurt you. I ask for your forgiveness. I know that I have been very defensive in this area. You have tried to talk to me but I wouldn't listen. That has changed. From this point forward I want you to tell me the truth, and I promise you won't pay a price. I need your input and I value it."

This is the type of communication between couples that can do miracles in your relationship. When the walls of inner vows come down, spouses can connect on a much deeper level. We become free from the words that have invisibly tethered us to the pain of our past. We are free to go forward, and to enjoy life and love as never before.

Time to Let Go

If you haven't dealt with any damaging inner vows you may be harboring, now is the time to do so. Surrender your pain to Jesus, and allow Him to be Lord of every area of your life. Give your spouse permission to speak into every area of your life.

Don't let the promises of the past keep you from the potential of your future. It's time to let go and move forward.

Chapter
seven

Yours, Mine, or Ours?

Years ago, I (Jimmy) counseled a newly remarried couple from our church. The wife had several children from her previous marriage, and the kids were creating a lot of problems for her new husband. They had been deeply affected by their parents' divorce, and were unwilling to accept their new stepfather.

I had known this man for many years, and he was a good, Christian man. I knew he would become a great husband and father if he were given the chance. But her children made life miserable for him. They were unwilling to accept him into the family, and would usually ignore anything he said.

Even worse, his new wife wouldn't do anything about it. Every time an issue would arise, she would take her children's side and not allow her husband to challenge her on it. She was constantly protecting her children from their new stepfather, and because of it, they showed him almost no respect.

When they came to me for counseling, he was at his wit's end. He couldn't understand why his new wife wouldn't allow him to parent her children. When I asked her about it, she let out a long sigh and said, "My kids have just been through so much already. Their father hurt them deeply, and I just can't allow them to be hurt again."

I asked her, "If you trusted him enough to marry him, why can't you trust him to help parent your children? You realize that this marriage will never work unless you allow him to be an equal parent to your kids, don't you?"

I went on to explain two of the laws of marriage found in Genesis 2:24. The first is the law of priority. Marriage has to take first place above children, work, and everything else. For the sake of the marriage, every other human relationship must take a back seat. Couples are commanded to leave their mothers and fathers and "cleave" to each other. You cannot bond with your spouse unless they hold the highest priority in your life. They will naturally resent anything or anyone that comes before them on your list of priorities. This is true in any marriage, including a blended one.

I also explained to her the law of possession. Genesis 2:24 says that in marriage, husbands and wives become "one." For that to happen, everything in the marriage must be shared. The only way two things can become one is through total surrender. This means when we come into marriage we must give everything we have to our spouse—including children from a previous marriage or relationship. It also means that we assume ownership of everything our spouse brings into the marriage, both assets and liabilities.

I explained to her that she had been breaking these two laws of marriage, and that their relationship would not work until she gave ownership of her children to her husband, and began making him her top priority. I told her that their family could only grow and succeed around the nucleus of a healthy marriage. And that her children—no matter how wounded—could only heal in the atmosphere of a secure and safe home. The laws of marriage create the safest home possible, and there are no exceptions to that truth.

After listening to all I had to say, she still couldn't do it.

She said to me, "I'm sorry, but I just can't do that to my kids. I can't allow them to be hurt again." And that was it. She had made up her mind and refused to change it.

I knew the minute they left my office that their marriage wouldn't survive. And I was right. Shortly afterward, they decided to divorce. I just wish that I could have somehow gotten through to her.

His or Hers?

In a traditional first marriage, husbands and wives come into the relationship with no children, and the entire focus of the marriage is on each other. There are no distractions to keep them from immersing their lives into getting to know each other on an intimate level.

Bonding is easy and natural, because all they have is each other. Then after a while, they decide to have kids. There is never any question about whose children they are, or who favors who. It is a very natural and organic process.

But in blended families, things aren't always that easy. In blended families, you have children, and then you try to introduce a marriage into the mix. The relationships between parents and children are already established, and then suddenly there is a new parent in the house. It's common for kids to feel a little jealous or apprehensive.

When couples remarry, it is common for parents to favor their biological children, and to instinctively try to protect them from their new stepparent. Often a wife will bring two or three children into the marriage, and she's seen her kids wounded deeply by the pain of her previous divorce. It was pain that she couldn't protect them from at the time, but afterward, her primary focus becomes keeping them from ever being hurt again.

He may bring several kids into the marriage as well, and they, too, have been wounded by his previous divorce. He is just as protective of his kids as she is of hers. And when they come together to blend their families, there are divided loyalties on every side. It's a very natural reaction, and a common theme in blended families. But it can deeply damage or even destroy a marriage if it isn't changed.

Kids who have lost a father to divorce many times don't want a new father. In their minds, they already have one. They're just upset that he doesn't live with them anymore. They will always love their "real" father, and struggle to accept a new one.

Kids who have been separated from their biological mother, whether it was through divorce or death, have lost a deeply integral part of their lives. They will always miss their "real" mother, even if she wasn't the best mother to them. There is a primal bond that happens during birth that can never be erased. Their love for their mother is woven into the fabric of their DNA. And when a new mother tries to step in and take her place, it can feel
devastating to them.

Most children will instinctively reject anyone who tries to take the place of their biological parent. And when parents enable this natural tendency by taking sides, or not allowing the new stepparent to share the role of parenting, it creates a level of tension and chaos that can quickly compromise the new marriage.

A United Front

In healthy blended families, parents understand this natural favoritism that children have toward their biological parent, and they don't try to force themselves on their stepchildren or replace their biological parents. They instead show a united front, but allow the biological parent in the home to be the primary disciplinarian—at least until the kids begin to feel comfortable taking correction from their stepparent.

This is especially important when children are older, and as they reach the teenage years. If a husband brings children into the marriage, he should be the one to dole out discipline and correction. This allows his new wife to instead focus on just loving the kids, and gaining their trust. His children already see him as their primary authority, so it's natural to them that he would be the one to correct them when they get out of line.

Obviously, his wife still must have equal authority over the children and be able to discipline them if necessary. The children cannot see her as helpless or subservient. She must have an equal voice regarding the children, and just as much authority in their lives. Otherwise, problems are sure to develop.

When a mother brings kids into a marriage, she should make it clear to them that her new husband has complete authority over them. And they should see her consulting him in every decision. But when it comes to implementing discipline or correction, she should take the primary role at the beginning.

Kids seldom question the love and authority of their biological parent, so again, it is that parent who should take the primary role when it comes to administering discipline. But this only works when both parents make it clear that they are not taking sides. A united front is critical in all situations, and especially when it comes to matters involving the children.

Kids have an uncanny ability to sense when their parents are not united on an issue. And when they are already struggling to accept the new marriage, they will use any areas of disunity to their advantage. They will play parents against each other, and do everything in their power to cause an argument or dissension in the ranks. And once they realize how easy it is to divide their parents, they will continue to do that each time they have an opportunity. I've seen so many blended families damaged, and even destroyed by children who simply refused to accept their new parent. I've also seen parents who were so protective of their own children that they found themselves constantly in conflict with their new spouse in an effort to keep the kids from getting hurt. But in reality, it was creating an environment that continued to hurt them.

It is a simple formula—if an unhealthy marriage hurt them, a healthy one can heal them. Prioritizing your marriage and sharing everything with your spouse honors the timeless and universal laws of marriage. It creates an atmosphere of security and safety. And even though the children may not understand that, it is up to the parents to do the right thing and be an example to them. Don't let pain or fear control your home. By faith, honor God's laws of marriage, and He will bless and honor you for it.

For blended families to work, it is critical that parents put the marriage first, in all situations. No matter what areas of conflict or struggle arise, the parents need to come together and agree on the best course of action. And then make sure the children know that they are in complete agreement. There can't be even a hint of discord between them—at least in the eyes of the children.

Even when their biological mother is the one implementing the discipline, children should know that their stepfather has that same authority. He is simply allowing his wife to take the primary role of disciplinarian out of respect for their feelings.

And the same goes for his biological children. Their father may be administering the discipline, but his wife has just as much say and authority over their lives as he does.

When parents are diligent and consistent in implementing this strategy within a new blended family, they soon discover that "blending" becomes much more natural and successful. Before long, the kids will usually begin to accept the advice and correction of their stepparent as easily as they do their biological one.

The Need For Modesty

There is another parenting dynamic that is somewhat unique to stepfamilies, and this one is much more sensitive and unspoken. But it's a very real issue that families need to deal with and discuss.

In biological families, there are natural sexual barriers in place between parents and their children, and even between siblings of the opposite sex. When the family is healthy, there are no unnatural attractions within the family to deal with.

But in stepfamilies, that dynamic changes. You are introducing members of the opposite sex into a family unit, and those natural sexual barriers have not been there from birth. That's especially true when kids are in their teen years, or approaching puberty.

I (Frank) have a vivid memory of something I witnessed in my early twenties that felt completely inappropriate to me. I was working in a bakery at the time, and a new co-worker asked me to pick him up for work one day when his car was in the shop. I knew that he had just married a divorced woman with several small children, though I had never met his new family. When I rang the doorbell, his wife answered and told me he was still in the shower. She invited me into the living room, where she introduced me to her three small children. They were precious young kids, ranging between the ages of three and ten.

We made small talk for a few minutes, and I could hear shuffling coming from the bathroom to one side. Then suddenly the door opened and my coworker appeared in the doorway, still drying off from his shower. He was completely naked, and barely covered up by a white towel. He apologized for running late and said he'd be dressed in a minute, then scurried down the hallway into their back bedroom. As he walked, all three of the kids turned to watch him, his naked bottom completely exposed to everyone.

It was bad enough that I had to look at his skinny backside, but the thought of these three children watching their stepfather wander around the house naked seemed highly inappropriate to me. In fact, I would consider it unfitting in any family, much less a blended one. I was completely taken back by the whole scene, yet it seemed perfectly normal to both him and his new wife. Neither seemed embarrassed or uncomfortable about it.

Just the same, it was highly inappropriate—and dangerous—and they both should have had more common sense.

When blended families come together under one roof, parents should immediately implement an added measure of modesty in the home. And it's something that needs to be openly discussed with everyone involved. This is especially true when children of the opposite sex are being integrated as stepbrothers and stepsisters. The natural barriers to sexual and physical attraction are not there, so discretion needs to be taught and practiced by every member of the family. This means parents and children need to wear robes, pajamas, or appropriate clothing around the house, and everyone need to dress and undress behind closed doors.

This isn't prudish advice, just prudent, given the reality of the situation. The point isn't to create an atmosphere of mistrust. It is to create an atmosphere of understanding and safety.

A Healthy Hierarchy

Integrating two families into one is rarely—if ever—easy, and it brings a host of issues that you might never have expected or imagined. Many times children appear to be completely in favor of the relationship before the wedding, but then once the family starts to blend, they realize how different things are going to be, and their natural instinct is to rebel and fight the changes.

Other times, you may find different "camps" forming within the family. Perhaps his children bond together and choose to ignore her kids during playtime. Or maybe the older kids pick on their younger stepsiblings. Or two half-siblings become jealous and competitive of each other, putting the family in a constant state of conflict.

Sometimes people simply have trouble connecting with a new stepchild, and you can't quite put your finger on the reason. So they begin to avoid each other, and do their best to stay out of each other's way. But this can't go on for long before causing hurt feelings on every side.

Conflict within a stepfamily has to not only be acknowledged, but dealt with openly and honestly. You can't ignore personality conflicts and hope they will somehow work themselves out. That's true whether the conflict is between husband and wife, parents and stepparents, natural siblings, or stepsiblings. Anytime personality conflicts arise within the family, the only healthy approach is to deal with it head on. And if you can't do it on your own, you have to be willing to bring in a qualified counselor or pastor to help your family work through it.

For families to truly "blend," it takes an intentional level of work and effort on the part of everyone involved. And as parents, it is our responsibility to see that every conflict is dealt with promptly and appropriately.

In healthy blended families, children are never seen as his or hers; they are always "ours." And the chain of command should be the same as it is in any traditional family unit.

God created families with a healthy sense of hierarchy, and that's the only approach to building a strong family unit. That's true whether the family is a traditional one, or a blended one.

Chapter
eight

Ex-Spouse-tations

I (Jimmy) have a distant relative who divorced a number of years ago, and soon afterward married into a blended family. Her second husband was a likeable and loving man who treated her much better than her first husband. We all liked him, and had high hopes for their marriage.

At the time, he was paying child support monthly to his ex-wife, since she had primary custody of the children. They had several kids, so the support he provided was a rather large amount. But he was a good man, and never missed a payment.

For some reason, my relative deeply resented this arrangement. From the moment they married, it was her biggest complaint, and she never quite got used to the idea. Every time he wrote out his child support check she would become angry and resentful. It was something they argued about on a regular basis, although I'm not sure what she expected of him. They were his children, and it was his responsibility to see that they were cared for financially. She should have been glad that her husband had such a strong sense of responsibility, but that's not how she chose to see it. She instead allowed the issue to become a huge source of contention between them.

Several of my relatives talked to her about it, but always to no avail. She continued to resent the child support payments her husband made, and it became a constant source of struggle in their marriage. They eventually divorced, and though I'm sure there were other factors involved, this issue was always their primary source of conflict. In reality, it wasn't the money that upset my relative so much. It was the fact that there would always be this third person involved in their relationship. Because of her husband's children from his previous marriage, she thought his ex-wife would always be an emotional and financial drain on their family, and that's what she resented the most.

Dealing With an Ex Spouse

In almost every blended marriage, there is one glaring issue that hangs over the marriage like a cloud. It is a "day one" dynamic that can't be ignored, and refuses to go away. In almost every blended marriage, there are ex-spouses somewhere in the picture. And because children are involved, those ex-spouses will always play a role in the dynamics of your family.

You will probably at some point be tied to them financially, either through shared property, or through alimony payments. You will be tied to them physically, because of their shared interest in your children. You will be tied to them emotionally, because they will always want to have some say in how the children are raised. And you will be tied to them spiritually, because they have open communication with your children, and are able to pass on values and ideas that you may not always appreciate or agree with.

In many circumstances, having an ex-spouse in the picture can be a challenge to the marriage, and detrimental to the health of the family unit. Yet it is something that you have to deal with, because when your children have another biological parent in the world, that relationship has to be respected.

I've pastored and counseled many blended families through the years, and have seen a lot of pain and distress brought on because of ties to a combative or immoral ex-spouse. It is one of the most difficult and frustrating issues that many blended families have to face.

One remarried couple came to me a few years ago agonizing over an issue that they were having with a bitter and ungodly ex-husband. The husband had shared custody of her three children, so they spent every other weekend with their father and his new wife. And their home was completely void of any spiritual or moral training.

Each time the kids spent time with their father, they would be exposed to things that their mother would never allow them to see. Their father would let them watch immoral and inappropriate movies, late into the evening hours. More than that, he would encourage it. And the conversations they would have over meals were never healthy or suitable for children.

Often he would use his time with the kids to try and turn them against their mother. He would mock her faith, and undermine her spiritual values. And he would grill them about her new marriage, and the things that went on in their home. He was a terrible influence on his children, and was still bitter and angry toward his ex-spouse, and would use the opportunity to undermine her authority at every turn. This mother came to me in tears pleading for some kind of help. She saw the damage her ex-husband was doing to her children, yet because of their shared custody, there was nothing she could do about it. She was legally obligated to let her kids stay at his home on a regular basis.

It was distressing to hear her story, and to know that there was nothing she could do to keep her kids away from their father. My heart broke for them both, because I knew how hard they were working to raise moral and godly children. I tried to imagine how I might react under similar circumstances. I can't imagine the pain they were experiencing, knowing that their children were being negatively influenced by someone they didn't want or need in their lives, yet there was nothing either of them could do about it.

Steps to Maintaining Peace

This is an issue I've seen time and again when couples in blended marriages come to me for counsel. And no two situations are ever quite the same. Sometimes it is an unhealthy ex-wife trying to undermine the family. Other times it may be an ex-spouses' wife or husband causing problems. Or maybe an unruly and obstinate child that lives with an ex-spouse but spends weekends at home, bringing unwanted trouble and conflict into the family.

In blended families, there are often many players involved, leaving room for a whole host of interpersonal complications. It takes a lot of wisdom and patience to navigate the many problems that can arise.

Because of that fact, there is no one-size-fits-all set of solutions for dealing with an ex-spouse. The dynamics are simply too complicated and varied to come up with one. But there are some practical, concrete principles and attitudes you can practice in order to minimize the trouble an ex-spouse can cause.

Some of these principles are easier to practice than others, but all are important to maintaining a truly mature and peaceful mentality in front of your children.

Never communicate through your children.

One of the biggest mistakes that couples make on the heels of divorce is using their children as unwilling—and reluctant—go-betweens as they attempt to communicate or "spy" on each other.

When a husband leaves his wife to marry a woman ten years her junior, it can be a humiliating experience. It can be devastating to her self-esteem. So she subconsciously begins using her children to spy on her ex-husband and his new "trophy wife." She begins grilling them for every detail. She wants to know what kind of clothes she wears, how she spends her day, how she spends her husband's money, where she gets her hair done, even her private habits and hang-ups. The last thing the children want to do is talk about their father's new wife, but their mother becomes obsessed with jealousy, and they are stuck in the middle.

A man whose wife divorced him because he was deceptive and unfaithful may know in his heart that he was the reason their marriage failed, yet still he resents his wife and her new husband. And he uses the children to get back at them. He spoils them every time they come to his house, and allows them to do anything their immature hearts desire, just so that he will be seen as the "fun" parent. His wife is forced to be the bad cop, because her ex-husband refuses to enforce her rules. And then she has to listen to her kids complain because "Daddy lets us stay up late," while she insists that they get in bed at a decent hour.

Most divorced parents are guilty of communicating with their ex-spouses through their children. They know it's wrong, but the temptation is just too great.

A mother is helping her kids pack for a weekend with their father, and she says to them, "Tell your dad I don't appreciate him being late with his child support payments again." Even as the words leave her mouth, she knows how wrong it is to bring them into her battles. But anger and resentment cloud her better judgment. She continuously finds herself saying things she shouldn't say.

It's a natural urge, but one that we must fight, if for no other reason, than for the sake of our children's mental health and stability. When kids have already been put through the pain of divorce, the last thing they need is even greater conflict and confusion. And they certainly don't need the agony of having to choose sides in an argument.

If you have something to say to your former spouse, the only healthy approach is to contact them on your own. Never communicate through your children.

Never compete for your children's attention or affections.

Another mistake many divorced people make is trying to compete with their ex-spouse for their children's loyalties.

A father may learn that his ex-wife is trying to serve healthier meals at home, so he counters it by loading up his fridge with ice cream, cookies and junk food. In his effort to be the favorite parent, he lets them eat whatever they want.

Or maybe he is jealous of his ex-wife's new husband, and wants to prove to his kids that he is the one who loves them most. So he tries to buy their affection. The minute his son shows an interest in golf, he showers him with all the latest gear and equipment, and even buys lessons with the local golf pro. He breaks the bank trying to prove that he's the better father.

This is a common reaction on the heels of divorce, but extremely unhealthy for the children. It not only confuses them, it encourages poor behavior and split loyalties. Kids can easily become spoiled and greedy, and learn to use their parents' compulsive anger to get what they want.

In the short run, kids almost always respond to bribes and payoffs, but that's a guaranteed formula for raising a card-carrying brat. What kids most need from their parents are clear boundaries, enforced rules, discipline, and unconditional love. If they can't get that from both biological parents, you can at least make sure that they get it from you.

Set clear boundaries with your ex-spouse.

Many conflicts between divorced couples are caused because boundaries of behavior are never discussed or implemented. A father may feel free to drop by his ex-wife's house unannounced whenever he wants, simply because his children are there. Or a mother may think she has the right to call her ex-husband at work when she needs to discuss a parenting or financial issue. And all parents think that they should be able to call their kids whenever they feel the need, even if they don't have full custody.

But there's a reason that courts set clear boundaries regarding visitation, child support payments, and contact with the children. Because without these boundaries, chaos and conflict are inevitable. And kids are always caught in the middle.

For the sake of your kids, and sanity in your home, it's critical that some clear physical and emotional boundaries are not only discussed, but enforced. And this includes boundaries that may or may not be part of your court-ordered separation.

Since all situations are different, only you and your ex-spouse can decide what these boundaries should be, or how they should be implemented and enforced. And you can't always expect your ex to cooperate the way you might hope. But it's important enough to try.

If you haven't done so already, I encourage you to make an appointment with your ex-spouse to calmly and openly discuss the matter in detail. Your new spouse should be included, and so should theirs, but only the adults should attend. And everything you discuss should revolve around what is best for the children, not your personal wants or complaints. If you need to bring in an impartial mediator, be willing to do so. The goal is to set clear and defined boundaries when it comes to the children, and their interests should trump any demand or complaint you might have.

If you have developed a habit of complaining about your ex-spouse to your children, this is your opportunity to confess that sin, and to ask your ex for forgiveness. And to promise you'll do whatever it takes to stop this damaging and negative habit. It's also a good time to ask if they are willing to make the same commitment.

If you and your ex-spouse have been competing for your children's affections, this is a good time to bring the matter up, and to try and reach a healthier, more mature balance when dealing with the children.

Whatever issues you and your ex-spouse are dealing with, the best approach to solving the problem is through calm and mature discussion. Be willing to take kind and humble steps toward open lines of communication for the sake of your children, and pray for an open spirit on the part of your ex-spouse.

Cover your children in prayer.

At the end of the day, there is nothing greater you can do for your children than to cover them in prayer on a daily basis. This is true regardless of your situation, or any negative influences that might be coming against them.

All children today are under a great deal of stress and temptation, and they all need the Holy Spirit's covering and protection in order to make wise life choices. But kids who have been through divorce often need an extra measure of grace and spiritual help.

Living in a blended family brings many unique challenges and hurdles, but when you have biological parents that can't seem to get along, those difficulties are often amplified to an unbearable level. The devil never lets a good crisis go to waste, and he never misses an opportunity to create even more pain and confusion in the heart of a child.

The good news is, God is more powerful than any crisis life may bring our way. And He is able to overcome even our greatest challenges or heartaches. God will protect your children from any negative spirits, words, or emotions that come their way if you stay on your knees and continue to cover them in prayer.

If you are struggling with animosity and anger toward an ex-spouse, God can heal your heart. Just confess your struggles and allow Him to begin to work.

If your children are being confused or tempted by the actions of an ex-spouse, pray that God would protect their innocent hearts and keep them from harm. If your kids are seeing things they shouldn't see, talk to them about it, and pray with them daily that God will give them strength to do the right thing, in spite of the temptations they might feel.

Prayer is the most powerful weapon we have against the devil's schemes, and we should wield it like a mighty sword in battle. In doing so, we're not only invoking the power of God in our lives, but we're setting an example for our kids that will carry them through any struggle, and stay with them for an eternity.

Never underestimate the power of prayer, or God's ability to overcome evil with good. Let it be your greatest source of comfort, and your first line of defense, no matter what struggles your family may be experiencing.

I tell parents in difficult situations with their exes to be thankful for every day their children are in their home. If the kids are being exposed to things they shouldn't see or hear, I encourage them to have faith that the atmosphere of their own home will have a greater impact than the permissive or ungodly atmosphere of their ex-spouse's. Don't underestimate the power of God or the sensitivity of your child's heart.

Even if kids enjoy being in a more permissive environment, they feel more safe in a home with clear boundaries and godly behavior. Have faith that God will honor you for your obedience, and that your children will ultimately choose your values over those less godly and devout.

Section Two

Secrets of Successful Stepfamilies

Chapter

Beginning to Blend

Trust is the backbone of a marriage relationship. When you have trust, you feel free to experience the full potential of your marriage partnership.

Trust brings intimacy, love, confidence, and vulnerability to a relationship. It allows you the freedom to be completely open and honest about your needs and desires, your dreams and fears, your future hopes and past failings. When you trust someone, you are able to share your heart and soul with them, because you know that what you share will be treasured and valued.

If marriage were a house, trust would be the foundation. It is the cornerstone that anchors and supports the entire framework of the relationship. It is the base upon which all other marital needs and desires are built. And trust is critical to every aspect of a marriage—finances, communication, commitment, faith, accountability, and everything else couples need to survive.

And trust is built at the very beginning of a relationship. It is just as important before marriage as it is after. Without it, you are setting yourself up for a lot of pain, stress, and turmoil.

When we asked our panel of eighteen successful stepfamilies about the most critical aspects of growing a healthy and happy blended family, trust was at the top of the list. And it was something they knew they needed to establish at the start of their relationship in order for their family to survive. For many of them, it was a violation of trust that caused their first marriages to end, and they had no intention of letting it happen again.

Learning to Trust Again

"Sometimes I think people are just afraid to put their heart out there and give one hundred percent trust … especially in subsequent marriages," explained Richard. "Because you've been hurt before, and you don't want to get hurt again."

Richard and his wife Sheri had both been married before, and had each experienced a lot of pain and heartache in their previous relationships. They had an intimate understanding of the damage caused when trust is breached, so they committed early in their dating relationship to building a strong foundation of open and honest communication.

Michael and Terry echoed their response. "During our dating season we were very forthright and transparent about our past and what we had been through, and I think that helped us gain that trust," said Michael.

Terry agreed with him. "His being very open, which normally would have scared me to death, actually proved to be a very positive thing in our relationship. He wasn't trying to sugarcoat anything, or make anything sound better than it was. And I think that really helped me to trust."

Will and Wanda had both been married twice in the past before they started dating, and each had a host of deep-seated trust issues to overcome in order for their marriage to work. They knew from the outset that it would be an uphill battle, but were committed to making their relationship last.

"I had some really strong barriers up," confessed Wanda, "It was really hard for me to be open and honest."

And Will had many of the same fears. "We both had baggage coming into this … I was hypersensitive to deceit and manipulation. So I just naturally thought that any person I dated was going to try to control me, or lie to me, or try to deceive me … I had to relearn how to trust."

Couples who have been through a failed relationship almost always come into remarriage with a heightened sense of fear and insecurity, and it takes an extra measure of trust to help them work through it. Any hint of deceit or dishonesty will immediately raise red flags. And deception is the last thing a person needs when trying to trust again.

The one point that our panel agreed on unanimously is the need for complete openness and honesty during the dating season, and well into the marriage relationship. This is true in any marriage, but especially critical for couples who are marrying for the second or third time.

Helping Children Through the Transition

In a blended family, children also tend to come into the relationship with a heightened level of doubt and insecurity, and often will have many of the same trust issues as their parents. They, too, have likely been wounded by the breakup of their family, and need help overcoming their fears. Kids are seldom equipped to process the emotions they are experiencing, and it takes a special level of sensitivity to help them work through it.

"Preparing your child for the merge of a blended family is very difficult," says Ty. Though her husband Charles had never been married, Ty brought a young son into their relationship, and her son was already struggling with issues of rejection and abandonment. She and Charles knew how fearful and wounded he had become, and so they included him in their relationship at every opportunity.

"I think the number one key is communication," Ty explained. "Communicating to the child what it's going to look like, and then talking through it with them."

"I did a lot of talking and listening," said Renee. "You know, asking them questions about how they felt, what were they thinking. When we actually started planning our wedding, I let them be involved in picking things … making them a part of the whole process."

Kids feel more secure when they know they have a voice, and that their opinion matters. When families make the decision to blend, it has a profound effect on the lives of the children involved. If they feel overlooked or ignored, it will have a marked impact on the success of the blending process.

"I think one of the most important things in helping children transition into a new family is understanding that you don't decide their relationship with the new parent, or with their new siblings," explained Andi. "It's not up to you. They're going to form that on their own, in their own time, and in their own way."

For a blended family to work, children need to feel the freedom to connect naturally and organically. If it feels forced or arranged, the relationship will tend to be strained and artificial.

"In our case, we had one child who could not stand him for a long time," said Jesi. "What we did is allow her to feel that way. We didn't try to force it. We didn't try to push her to like my husband. We let that happen naturally."

Today, Jesi's daughter and her new husband Paul are closer than they ever imagined they would be. And that might have never happened if they had tried to force her to accept him. Their daughter knew that the decision was hers, and that made all the difference in how she responded.

Children also need to know that the new marriage won't alter or implode their relationship with their own parent.

Craig and April brought six children into their marriage, so they knew they had a special set of challenges to overcome in this area. Craig consistently worked to reassure his kids of his commitment toward them as a father. "I'm still your dad, and I'm going to be your dad no matter what," he told them.

And April reassured them as well. "I'm not taking him away from you," she told them. "[Your] relationship will still be there. Hopefully it will be stronger than it ever was."

One of the greatest challenges that couples face when blending two families into one is helping the kids stay onboard with the process. And often it takes a great deal of flexibility and compromise in order to help that happen. That willingness to bend and negotiate when the situation warranted it was a common trait we saw among our panel of successful stepfamilies. They were committed to making the process as smooth and painless as possible for their children, and willing to sacrifice their own needs and desires in order to make that work.

Bonding as a New Stepfamily

Helping children adjust to a new stepfamily is an important step in the process, but it's only the first step. For blended families to succeed, there needs to be a consistent and ongoing emphasis on growing and bonding as a family. The ultimate goal is to create a family unit that no longer feels like "his" children or "her" children, but just another healthy, happy, traditional family. "As we were married and began blending as a family, we would have a date night every week," explained Renee. "We established game nights where we would have family time. We made sure to schedule family vacations. It was an inclusion process."

Renee brought two daughters into the marriage, and had been a single mom since both were young, so she understood how difficult it might be for them to accept Scott as their father. In order to help them bond, they set out to create intentional times of fun and togetherness. They took vacations to Scott's hometown so they could see where he grew up, and then took the kids to meet his parents. She wanted her kids to connect with her husband on an emotional level in order to help them accept him as their new father.

Moises and Maggie had many of the same challenges, though it went both ways, since they each brought children into their marriage.

"Coming in as a stepdad," said Moises, "I tried to create memories. I tried to create new memories with the kids. Not to outdate the old memories they had with their dad. But…so that they know I am here to stay, and that we're all in this together."

"Having been a single mom, and a working mom, I was always running," said Maggie. Often she would grab meals on the run with her children. They seldom sat down to eat at the table for a meal. But when she and Moises married, they decided to change that pattern. In order to help her kids bond with their new father, they began eating dinner together as a family every night. It was a new tradition for her children, but something they quickly came to enjoy and anticipate. It was a simple thing, but important to the bonding process.

Philip was a single father when he met Valenceia, so in order to help his son accept their new marriage, he took great pains to spend intentional time alone with his son. It was actually Valenceia's idea.

"We called it "Father-Son" day," says Philip. And it happened every Tuesday night. Sometimes they would go to a movie, other times they would go to dinner, or on a long walk.

"We made sure that time was our time," he said. "A time that was just me and him, where he had a chance to express himself and to talk and just have fun with his dad. Just to let him know that he was still a priority in our lives."

When helping kids bond into a new blended family, there are no one-size-fits-all set of rules, because all children have different needs and expectations. The key is to understand the struggles your kids may be having, and deal with them on an individual basis. It takes time, patience, and creativity. And it takes an extra measure of love and sensitivity. But with the right attitude and commitment, any blended family can create a safe, happy, and unified environment in the home.

Establishing Right Priorities

"From the classes that I've been through," explained Michael, "I learned personally to put God first, your spouse second, your children third, and your work fourth. I think keeping those priorities in check has really helped me grow as a husband and father."

His wife Terry reiterated that sentiment. "Actually, I keep that on a sticky note," she said. "Having that list keeps it very real for me … That's something that keeps me directed and on target."

Keeping right priorities is difficult in any marriage relationship, but especially challenging in a blended family. The inherent "day one" dynamics of a stepfamily create a lot of room for chaos and turmoil, making it hard to keep your focus on what's truly important. But regardless of the challenges, it is critical to the success of your family to keep priorities in proper order. And God's priority is that the marriage always comes before any other human relationship.

"Our behavior and our mindsets totally had to shift," explains Charles, "and we had to really reprioritize mentally."

As the single parent of a young boy, his wife Ty had always put her son first. He was the center of her universe. But when Charles came along, all that had to change. The marriage had to suddenly become her top priority, and it was a tough transition for all of them. But she understood God's design for marriage, and knew that she had to change her way of thinking for the relationship to survive.

Jesi had to make that same change of mindset when she married Paul.

"You've now chosen this person as your spouse," she said. "You've made a commitment before God that this is the person you're going to live the rest of your life with. There is a priority that's biblical, and if we don't live by that priority, we're cheating our relationship with our husband. Yes it is our job—and definitely our honor—to raise [our children] up in the way they should go, but they are going to grow and move away. And we still need to maintain and grow our relationship."

"That was part of the reason why my first marriage failed," says Velory, "because my husband wasn't a priority. My children were. I realized that that was one of my errors."

Velory knew when she married Bryan that those priorities would have to change. So she committed to putting God first, Bryan second, and everything else behind that. It is the primary reason their blended marriage has been so rewarding and successful.

"I would definitely say that being able to go to the Lord first in all of our decisions has made the difference in this marriage," says Velory.

In a marriage relationship, anything that comes before your spouse will create tension and resentment. If your career is your highest priority, your spouse will resent your job. If golf or football or baseball is your highest priority, your spouse will feel neglected and jealous of every moment you spend playing and talking about sports. If your children are your highest priority, your spouse will come to resent the time you spend with them, even if they love your kids as much as you do.

The first priority of marriage is that the marriage always has to come first. Only your relationship with God is more important.

Children thrive in an environment of safety and security, and the safest place they can be is in a home with two parents who put each other first, in every circumstance. If it was a broken marriage that hurt your children, it's a healthy marriage that will help them heal. They don't need your constant doting and attention. They need stability. They need a healthy and secure home in which to grow. They need parents who are happy and committed to each other and to the marriage relationship.

If you give that to them, you're not only freeing them from any fears and insecurities they may have brought into your blended family, but also setting an example for them to follow in their own future marriage.

Chapter

ten

Overcoming Damaged Emotions

" I thought that when I had married Charles I was good," Ty explained. "I had forgiven, I had said my prayers, I extended forgiveness, and I had cried my tears … Until he touched a spot that was hurting. Or until he did something that reminded me of something my ex-spouse had done. Then I realized, 'I guess I haven't forgiven. I guess I'm not healed.' I really thought that it could happen overnight—that I could make the decision and move on. But it was a journey... A lot of things I had to get over. A lot of things I had to let go."

All marriages have to deal with pain and baggage from past hurts and relationships. We are flawed and sinful people, and we live in a fallen world. Even young couples entering into marriage for the first time are going to experience turmoil because of past wounds and damaged emotions. Those wounds may come from a painful childhood, parents, siblings, an old girlfriend or boyfriend, even an ex-boss or a schoolteacher that didn't like us. Whatever pain we carry will likely surface once we begin building a life with another person.

But blended families usually have an even greater degree of stress and tension to deal with. By their very nature, remarriages are riddled with much more baggage from past relationships, and wounds that are likely much deeper and more pronounced.

That's why many second marriages end in a second divorce. Because so few couples are prepared for the issues they are likely to experience, or equipped to handle the fragile and damaged emotions when they begin to surface.

Dealing With Past Pain

"As the new spouse in a blended family," said Charles, "I think it's important that you understand your role from day one. And a part of your role will be—not may be, but will be—to help them heal. To establish new trust, new belief, new hope in relationships. And to help them process in a really gracious and understanding way."

Patience and acceptance are important in any new marriage, but especially critical when you know your spouse is struggling with past wounds and insecurities. It takes a special measure of love and commitment to bring healing to a damaged heart. And that's something you can give your spouse that they can't get from any other human relationship.

Marriage is about learning to extend grace. And learning to receive it when you are the one who is hurting.

This is a fundamental trait of any successful blended family. Healthy couples learn to lean on each other in tough times, instead of lashing out.

"When we came into this relationship, we both had a lot of past hurts," says Sheri. "And I think we were trying to deal with them on our own a lot at the beginning. But … we finally started talking to each other about it. Now, after years of doing it the wrong way, we just have these really long and deep conversations with each other, where we ask questions of each other."

Sheri and her husband Richard had each been married before, and both came into their new marriage with a deeply painful past. They didn't always handle conflict well. But in time they learned the importance of open and honest communication. And honesty has a way of fostering a much greater level of compassion, grace, and intimacy.

"You can't be afraid of conflict," said Sheri. "Without conflict there is no growth. And blended families are going to have conflict. You're going to have trial and error. You're going to get back up, dust yourself off, and you're going to be great, and then you're going to fall again. You just can't give up, because things are going to get better."

Past pain does more than create conflict. It also causes inner turmoil and self-hate. People who come into marriage with regret often have trouble forgiving themselves. And it's almost impossible to move forward until you truly put your past behind you.

"I've never had problems forgiving people," confessed Craig. "I have a problem forgiving myself." His wife April struggled with those same issues. "I think a lot of divorced couples blame themselves," she said. "So it's harder for them to continue to move on."

It's extremely common for divorced couples to struggle with issues of unforgiveness. They struggle to forgive themselves and their exes, and they struggle to feel forgiven by others. They also have a hard time accepting God's forgiveness. But forgiveness is a critical step in any healing process. Until we truly learn to embrace that we are loved and forgiven by God, regardless of our past, we will never be fully able to extend that grace to others.

Making Peace With the Past

Another critical step to moving forward is learning to make peace with our past, including anyone who may have hurt us—especially an ex-spouse or another previous relationship.

"One of the major ways I've been able to heal from the past," said April, "is I've really had to realize that my husband is not my ex-husband. Sometimes [I would] deal with situations in the same manner because of those past hurts." Like many remarried spouses, April had found herself transferring her anger toward her ex-husband onto her new husband Craig. And it took a conscious, concerted effort on her part to change that negative pattern of behavior.

"Making peace with your ex-spouse … needs to be a priority," says Ty. "Because if it's not a priority, it's definitely going to cause a wedge in the new relationship that you're building. You really have to extend forgiveness, regardless of what they did, regardless of the pain. You really have to release it."

And Will agreed with her. "When you're divorced, it's so easy to hate the other person. Especially when they're talking bad about you—from innuendos to blatant lies. One of the things I have to consciously tell myself is, 'This is somebody that God loves. This is somebody that God created, just like me.'"

The temptation to demonize an ex-spouse or a previous partner is always going to be there. Anytime a relationship ends, there are unprocessed wounds residing in the depths of our hearts. Especially if the relationship involved sexual intimacy. You can't just turn off resentment. You have to work through it. You have to find a way to forgive and move forward, no matter how difficult that may be.

And the more emotional ties you have, the longer it may take to get past them. But it's something that needs to be done in order for your new marriage to grow and develop. Not just for your sake, but for the sake of your children.

"[Your children] still want to see that you have some kind of relationship," explained April. "Because it hurts the kids when you're not together if they were used to you being together. They want to know that you have some kind of mutual understanding, or some kind of friendship, however that may look. Sometimes it's about swallowing your pride."

When marriages end, children don't always come away with the same feelings of resentment and anger as their parents might have toward each other. They are often left wondering why their parents had to separate, and why their family had to be torn apart. In most cases, children still have deep feelings for both of their parents, and they need to know that both parents still have feelings for them—even if they aren't living in the same home.

"The truth is that your spouse loved that person enough that they were married to them," said Scott, "and they had children with them. And whatever happened, you have to be secure enough in your relationship to help them through grieving the loss of that relationship."

When Scott married Renee, she had two daughters who both struggled deeply with the breakup of her first marriage. They missed their father, and the transition was difficult for them. So Renee and Scott had to work hard to reassure them that they would still have a relationship with their biological father. Renee explained to her daughters, "I love your dad, and I want good for him."

It was something her daughters needed to hear. And something that both she and Scott regularly remind them as they work toward growing a new blended family.

"I also think praying for your ex-spouse is important," said Jesi. "We both have done that … God can change a heart. I think it's important that you pray for them, and you ask God to change their heart. And if you need your heart changed, that you ask God to change your heart if there's anger or hurt or past wounds from that marriage."

Praying for those who have hurt us is one of the most important steps toward healing and forgiveness, so it was encouraging to hear this point from our panel of successful stepfamilies. It is a principle that I (Jimmy) have taught and practiced throughout my years of teaching and counseling. It is extremely difficult to harbor a grudge toward someone when you are actively praying blessings over their life and future. It's hard to stay mad at someone while you're asking God to bless them. And it's a critical step in truly moving forward.

When you hold a grudge, your grudge holds you. You are the one being held hostage to the offense, not the one who offended you. The only healthy approach is to learn to let it go, once and for all.

Dealing With the Stigma of Remarriage

"I think it's important for us to remember that our identity is not in the fact that we have a blended family," said Jesi. "For us, having a blended family is something that we treasure."

One of the most difficult aspects of living in a blended family is dealing with the stigma attached to divorce. There is still a measure of criticism and disapproval in the body of Christ toward stepfamilies. And even outside the church, there are lots of social stigmas to overcome. Blended families struggle to feel accepted and appreciated in many circles of society. But it's a stigma that healthy stepfamilies find a way to shake off in order to move forward.

"God hates divorce, but you know sometimes stuff happens," added Sheri. "We realize now that we probably could have stayed married to our previous spouses if we'd had the information that we have now. We talk about that all the time. But you can't unscramble eggs. It's harder being in a blended family than a regular family, but you can do it."

Her husband Richard nodded in agreement. "It's not what other people say about your marriage," he explained. "It's not what other people think from the outside about your marriage. It's what you and your spouse and God say about your marriage." Embracing God's love and forgiveness is a critical step toward developing a successful stepfamily, even if you feel judged by others. None of us can undo the past, and God doesn't expect that from us. God looks only to a bright future, and we need to learn to do the same.

"I would have to say that a blended family is a perfect example of God's redemption," said Renee. "Just like Pastor Jimmy says, 'This could be your eighth marriage, but if you do it God's way, it can be the marriage of your dreams.' It's so true. It doesn't matter what your past is. Blended families are the perfect example of how God can take what was so broken… and blend it perfectly together and make it very beautiful."

Chapter
eleven

Parenting and Discipline

Fairy tales haven't done much to help the image of stepparents. Many of us immediately think of the wicked stepmother or the evil stepfather when we imagine the modern day blended family. The stereotypes are strong, but it's not the reality that stepfamilies want to experience.

For blended families to work, parents have to learn to accept stepchildren as their own. And children must respect and obey both parents. A positive stepparent relationship is critical to the success of the family, and essential for a happy, harmonious household.

So how do you connect with your stepchildren as a parent and a friend? How do you learn to love a stepson or stepdaughter the same as your biological children? Is it possible to treat them all the same? And what should parenting and discipline look like in a healthy blended family?

Here's what our panel of successful stepfamilies had to say about parenting and discipline in a blended family:

Equal Commitment Versus Equal Love

"Honestly," said Renee, "how can you say that you love [your] stepchild the same as your biological child, when there has been so much more history? It would be hard to say that truthfully. But as far as your commitment to the best interest of that child, you have committed your life to [their] father, and that love and that commitment is going to help you always seek the best interest of that child."

Stepparents often set unrealistic expectations for themselves when it comes to bonding with their stepchildren. They think that they are supposed to have the same feelings for a stepchild as they do toward their biological children, so they tend to overcompensate. They may show their stepchild an inordinate amount of love and attention, trying to win their favor and rush the bonding process. But that can easily backfire and have the opposite effect.

The best approach is to let the process happen naturally. And to let your stepchildren set the pace for the relationship. If you allow them to bond in their own time, and in their own way, the relationship will grow at a healthier pace, and eventually be even stronger.

"For me," Renee continued, "with his kids, and with our adopted son, I can honestly say that I love those kids like my own. But it didn't happen overnight. I had to be committed to the process, and I had to be committed to what was in [their] best interest, even when I didn't understand what was going on with them."

In any healthy relationship, love is a determined act of the will. It isn't a feeling or something that just happens naturally. You have to work at it. You commit to the relationship, and determine to do what is in the best interest of the other person, even when you don't feel like it. That's true whether it's a marriage relationship, or a parenting one.

"I don't love my kids equally," said Sheri, "but I love them individually. I love them uniquely. I feel like it's across the board the same, but just in different ways, because they have different strengths, different things about them that you love."

Richard and Sheri both brought children into their marriage, and they had to learn to love each other's children as their own. And it was a process that happened over time. It wasn't something they could force or orchestrate. It happened through years of consistency and commitment.

J.D. and Andi had that same experience.

"If you expect your spouse to love every child—and treat every child—the same," said Andi, "you're constantly going to be saying, 'He's not doing it.' Because [that's] not possible. Even with my two biological children, I don't treat them exactly the same. They're different ages. They have different interests. They have different personalities.

I cannot possibly imagine loving them any more, but I don't treat them exactly the same."

"It's very difficult to love someone else's child the way that you love your own," confessed Jesi. "It's a different relationship. A mother's love is going to be different. I have committed to be the best parent that I can be to both of my children. And I know that they know that that's my commitment to them."

When learning to love a stepchild, our panel of successful stepfamilies was united on their advice in this area. The key to bonding is time, commitment, and allowing the process to happen organically. Forcing the issue can easily create tension in the family, and can even damage your relationship in the long run. Kids need time to accept their new parent, and it's important that we allow them room to bond in their own way.

Avoiding Stepsibling Rivalry

Stepchildren also need to learn to bond with each other. And that, too, may take time and patience. Anytime two families come together under one roof, jealousy and suspicion are bound to arise. Children may not like the idea of sharing their parent with another child, and they will be naturally protective and cautious. It is our job as parents to diffuse any feelings of resentment or distrust.

"I feel like you should encourage them to get to know each other," said Valenceia. "Encourage them to have a relationship with each other."

She and her husband Philip both brought young children into the marriage, and to help them bond as siblings, they intentionally left the children alone so that they could get to know each other better—not just as siblings, but as friends and playmates. Valenceia jokes that she would put them together in a room and close the door so that they had to play.

As parents, it's our responsibility to teach children how to treat each other, and how to interact as siblings. Getting along is a skill, and like any other skill, it needs to be taught and developed.

Charles had a firsthand perspective on the subject of sibling rivalry, since he grew up in a blended family. He remembers being jealous of his stepsister because of the added attention she got.

"When my stepsister would come, she would get all of the attention," he remembered. "They would take her shopping, and do all of these different things for her. And I'm sitting here like, 'I've been here every day and this doesn't happen for me!' I wasn't mature enough to understand that this [was] their limited time, and [they attempted] to make the limited time special."

From his experiences as a child, Charles learned firsthand the harm that can be done when parents appear to be playing favorites. It's an easy trap for stepparents to fall into—especially when another parent has joint custody. But it's a sure way to create tension and jealousy between stepsiblings.

"If you can spend individual time with each child," said Charles, "I believe it would … help to squash any sibling rivalries, or blended sibling rivalries. I think you also should sit down with both children and allow them to voice their opinions in a respectful way. Sit down and say, 'What do you think about this? How are we doing in this area?'"

As in all human relationships, communication is critical to overcoming sibling rivalry. When children aren't getting along, it's a mistake to remain silent and hope that things will naturally work themselves out. They will usually just get worse.

The best approach is to address the problem head-on and help children talk things through. Encourage them to discuss their feelings openly and truthfully, and then help guide them as they work to overcome any relational issues they may be having.

Kids are going to argue and disagree. So it's important not to overreact when they do. But it's also important to recognize ongoing problems of sibling rivalry, and to do whatever it takes to help kids get past it.

"One thing that I think helps to neutralize that competitiveness," said Shana, "is … to let them know that they as an individual are special … Nurturing their individual gifts lets them know that they don't need to compete with the next person, because they themselves are special. We look for what's special about them as individuals, and we try to draw that out of them."

Ultimately, children need what we all need. They need love, acceptance, and recognition. They need to know that they have a safe place to go whenever life gets tough and confusing. They need to know that they have two parents who love them for who they are, and accept them unconditionally. When children have that, other relationships will usually fall into place—even a strained relationship with a new sibling.

Guidelines for Discipline and Correction

"I know how my son feels when I discipline him," says Ty. "He's mad. He doesn't like it. And he loves me. I've been there from the beginning. So imagine how a child is going to feel when a stepparent steps in and tries to administer discipline."

Like a lot of new stepfamilies, Charles and Ty entered into marriage assuming that disciplining their son would be a role they shared equally. But they soon learned otherwise. Ty's son didn't like being corrected by his new stepfather. So they learned a better approach. Charles allowed Ty to be the primary disciplinarian, while he focused on getting to know his new stepson as a friend and buddy. He became the "good guy," while Ty doled out discipline and correction—at least until he got to know Charles better.

Today, discipline is a role they both share equally. And it works because they allowed it to happen naturally over the course of time.

Paul and Jesi had the same experience during the early years of their marriage. Often one of them would be disciplining their stepchild and the other would instinctively come to the child's defense. It's a natural reaction that parents have when they sense that their child's self image might be in danger of harm. They soon learned that it didn't work.

"It was not successful," Jesi says. "We found that, not only are you undermining [your spouse], but you're teaching your child lack of respect for the other parent. I wanted him to be a disciplinarian. I wanted him to be a father figure for my children … [but] I was just teaching the children that he had no value."

Whether dealing with kids in a traditional family or a blended one, the number one rule is to always show a united front. When kids sense that their parents are not on the same page when it comes to rules and discipline, they can easily capitalize on it, playing one parent against the other. It's an instinctive reaction, not necessarily a rebellious one. Children want to know where the boundary lines are drawn, and they will test those boundaries to find out.

As a general rule of thumb, new blended families should allow the biological parent to be the primary disciplinarian, but let it be known that both parents have equal authority in the home. And, that they both agree on what is and isn't acceptable behavior.

It's also critical that you not allow your children's other parents to undermine your authority.

"One thing that's important with discipline," explained Philip, "is not only my spouse and myself being on the same page, but also the child's mother, or their father … that they're on the same page. You want to let them know that this is how we're going to run our house—this is how we're going to discipline—so that there are no surprises."

One of the hardest aspects of sharing custody of your kids with another parent is maintaining consistency and stability when it comes to discipline and instruction. As a parent, you want to pass on your values and principles, and that's hard to do when another parent is in the picture, undermining your authority—whether purposefully or unwittingly.

If at all possible, the best approach is to openly communicate your wishes with your child's other parent. If you have concerns about the way they discipline, find a time to discuss it honestly. If they allow your kids to do things that you don't approve of, calmly talk about it with them, and see if you can come to a mutual compromise. Try to maintain a healthy relationship with your ex-spouse, and keep the lines of communication open. The focus should always be on what's best for the children, and that is hopefully the one thing on which any two parents can agree.

Dealing With Kids in Crisis

"Whenever you're dealing with a child in crisis in a blended family," advises April, "don't keep it hidden. Reach out. Reach out to a pastor or counselor… definitely do not keep it hidden… because breaking the rules is just a symptom of something deeper."

"If you're finding that your child is doing drugs, smoking pot, having sex, whatever it is … those are just symptoms to fill a hurt that's in their heart. And once you get down to the real issue of the problem, it's a lot easier for them to recognize it, and then for them to allow the Lord to start to heal that."

Children often come into blended families with a lot of hidden pain and anger from the past. If they experienced the breakup of their biological family, they are likely still harboring feelings of sadness and resentment. Kids seldom come through divorce unscathed or unaffected. And those scars can easily cause children to act out and rebel—especially as they get older.

During these phases of rebellion, what they most need is parents who love and accept them, no matter what they might be going through. Often it is you that their anger is directed toward—not because you deserve it, but because we always hurt the ones closest to us.

The best approach in these situations is to begin by spraying yourself with Teflon, and realize that it isn't really you they are mad at. Then deal with the problem head-on. Children who rebel, no matter what their age, need to know that their behavior is unacceptable. That's true in any family, not just a blended one.

If you don't know what to do, seek advice from a trusted counselor or mentor. But don't ignore the problem. And never assume it will work itself out in time.

Also, don't assume that the other parent is on the same page.

"If you have a kid that's in crisis," says Andi, "don't expect the other family to be handling it. A lot of times as a stepmother, I assume that the mother is handling the crisis … But you have to let go of that expectation … They may not even realize there's a crisis going on."

Ideally, when kids are in a stage of rebellion, all of their parental figures are united in how best to deal with it. But that isn't always the case. If you have an open dialogue with your child's other parent, try to discuss the issue and come to a mutual understanding of how best to handle it. Once again, if you keep the focus on what's best for the child, it shouldn't be that hard to find common ground. "If we don't deal with it now," said Pete, "we're going to have to deal with it at some point. And I'd rather deal with it at fourteen than [be] dealing with it at twenty-five."

When kids rebel, it's usually a cry for help. And anytime someone cries for help, they need someone there to hear them. As parents, it's our job to be our children's greatest ally, no matter what they might be going through.

A parent's most important role, whether raising a biological child or a stepchild, is to get them to adulthood with their faith intact and their reputation unharmed. And the best way to do that is to stay on your knees, and keep your wits and emotions in check. Pray daily for God to guide their hearts and minds. And for wisdom as you mentor them through times of crisis and turmoil.

The good news is, most kids who rebel eventually grow up to embrace their parents' spiritual values and beliefs. And when they do, they usually wonder why they fought so hard against it. So don't allow yourself to lose hope. Just hang on, and allow God room to work through you.

Chapter twelve

Inter-Relational Issues

Joint custody arrangements can be exhausting, especially after an acrimonious breakup. You have to get past any painful history you may have with an ex in order to negotiate important decisions. How do you arrange pick up and drop-off times? Where will kids spend the holidays? What about special occasions, vacations, birthdays, piano recitals, and other important events that involve the children? And how do you go about establishing rules and boundaries that everyone can agree on?

There's nothing about this type of co-parenting that is easy or ideal, but it's a reality that must be dealt with. Especially when mandated by the courts. The key is to focus entirely on the needs of the children, and keep their well-being at the center of every conversation and decision. Their desire is to maintain a close relationship with both sets of parents, and that should be both parents' desire as well.

All situations are different, so advice in this area is not as cut and dried as other areas we discussed with our panel of successful stepparents. But here's what they had to say about a number of ex-spouse issues they've had to deal with:

Navigating Joint Custody Issues

"You don't make the child a messenger," said Renee. "You don't send messages to the other parent through the child. If it's not a cordial relationship, write a note or letter, or whatever else you have to do, but I think it's important not to make the children a go-between. Those kinds of things just breed conflict, and more insecurity and fear."

"And more stress on the kid," added her husband Scott.

When your relationship with an ex-spouse is strained and tense, you don't always want to communicate with them any more than is needed, so it's tempting to let your children communicate for you. This is an easy habit to fall into, and far more convenient than trying to contact them on your own. But it's terribly stressful for the children. They don't want to run screen for parents that can't get along, and we should never allow ourselves to burden them with that responsibility.

If you have something to communicate to your ex, find a way to do it that doesn't involve the children.

It also helps to make joint custody as easy on the children as you can. The less stress you create, the better they will adjust to the idea of going back and forth between two families.

"One thing I did to help her when transitioning from home to home on weekends," said Wanda, "is I made sure she had everything at her dad's house that she would need, without having to pack a suitcase every time. I wanted it to be easy on her, and not make it such a huge ordeal going to dad's every other weekend."

Anything you can do to soften the stress of co-parenting is worth looking into. You might even ask your kids what you can do to make life easier for them as they go back and forth between homes.

Philip and Valenceia had a problem that comes up a lot in shared custody situations. Her ex-husband's wife would call on a moment's notice and ask to pick the kids up early for dinner or a special event. They wanted to be amicable, so they usually agreed. But it created a lot of undue hurry and stress. They would scramble to get things together, and then meet the other parent at a parking lot to pass off the children. It was getting to be a huge problem.

"It would be an inconvenience," Valenceia explained. "Either we would have to meet her, or we'd have to wait for her to come get him, and we never knew how much time that would be."

They eventually had to meet with her ex-husband and work out a better solution. They solved the problem by setting a clearly-defined schedule and then holding everyone to it.

Their advice to anyone in this same situation is simple but effective.

"You have to establish boundaries, so [you're] all on the same page, and can all live your lives in peace, and not running around like a chicken with his head cut off. You establish those boundaries, and you make sure you're consistent in sticking to them."

Most logistical issues of joint custody are pretty easy to solve with straightforward communication. When something is creating a problem, don't be afraid to sit down with your ex and talk it through. As always, if you keep the focus on what's best for the child, most reasonable parents will be willing to compromise.

Dealing With Negative Influences

"One of the things we've noticed," said Richard, "when you're dealing with a blended family and the kids have to go spend time with the other parent. When they come back, it seems like they're a different child. It's not the same child that you sent off. Sometimes that's hard to deal with, because you can't tell them that they can't spend time over there. You can't tell them that they can't go have visitation."

Ex-spouses don't always share our spiritual views and values, and sometimes they undermine our authority by ignoring the rules and guidelines we've set for our children. It's tough to parent with consistency when you have to share custody with a parent who isn't on the same page.

Craig and April had to deal with this dynamic firsthand. They often worried about what their kids might see or experience when they were with their other parent. They had to learn to fight the urge to grill their children, and instead trust God to guide their hearts and eyes.

"People in any relationship want to feel like they have control," explained Craig. "And you don't. You do not have control. What you have are boundaries, guidelines, and love. And you do the best you can. Just show them who you are, because it's all about example."

This was a parenting dynamic that several of our successful stepfamilies had to navigate. In each case, they had the same advice.

"You do the best you can," Richard explained. "and then when they come back home, you just love on them, and you just embrace them again... and realize that one day they're going to grow up, and they're going to come to their own conclusions and make their own mind up … So you have to have a lot of grace, a lot of mercy, and a lot of forgiveness when dealing with exes."

Scott and Renee agreed.

"I would just encourage parents who are sending kids into circumstances that may be challenging," advised Renee, "to coat everything in prayer. Lift them up the whole time they're gone, before they go … I think setting the moral standard in your home is key. And anything that you're concerned about, just encourage them in loving ways, without condemning the other parent."

Paul and Jesi reiterated those thoughts.

"When it comes right down to it," said Paul, "you want to let the child know, 'This is the rule in my house. I know you may do that at Mom's house, but this is how it works here.' We set some structure that I know they appreciate. When they go back and forth between houses, they thrive on that structure."

This is perhaps the most difficult dynamic that any parent will ever have to face. Yet because of the reality of shared custody agreements, many blended families have to deal with it on a daily basis.

"I used to stress about it every time he went over there," confessed Philip. "You know, 'What's happening over there? What's he exposed to? What kind of friends does she have over there? What kind of music, what kind of movies?' All those kinds of things."

Philip and his wife Valenceia were committed to instilling godly principles and values into their son, and they worried deeply about the time he spent with his biological mother. But worrying only added to the stress, so they instead focused on what they could control, instead of agonizing over what they couldn't.

"At the end of the day," Philip continued, "we don't do those things at our house. We're going to continue to have positive reinforcement with him. We're going to continue to show him, 'This is why we do this. This is why we don't allow you to watch certain things. This is why you don't get to listen to certain music … You may not understand it now, but one day you will make that choice, and hopefully it's the right one.'"

Instead of worrying, they put the matter to prayer. "We have to trust God," said Philip. "At the end of the day, when he's over there it's out of our hands. It's in God's hands.

When Adult Kids Reject Your Relationship

One hurtful dynamic that a lot of blended families have to deal with is adult children who refuse to accept the new relationship, and choose instead to pull away and reject the new spouse. They may still harbor feelings of anger and resentment over the divorce, and don't want to see either of their parents in a new relationship.

Several of the couples we talked to experienced this firsthand, including Craig and April. It was a painful dynamic for the family to overcome.

"I think that the most important thing is for you not to feel rejected," said Craig. "You have to be the adult. You're the parent … So even if they don't want to talk to you, or they don't want to see you, you can write them. You can text them. You just have to consistently do that. It does make a difference, even though they may not say it."

When Scott and Renee decided to marry, Scott's adult children never accepted their new relationship. But Scott understood that his first priority was to his wife, so they had to make some tough decisions.

"One of the things that I had to deal with a lot was guilt," said Renee, "because I felt like it was my fault that he couldn't have a relationship with his daughter. And it really was hard for me. I felt so guilty ... It used to just really eat me up."

The children's choice was hard on Scott, but he knew he had to remain loyal to Renee as his wife. He prayed that his kids would someday accept their new marriage.

"My encouragement for anyone who has to choose their spouse over their adult child," said Scott, "is to surrender that to the Lord. That's what we had to do. As hard as that is. We tried everything we could to reconcile that relationship, and to draw them in and include them ... If they ultimately are bent on dividing you, you have to choose your spouse and surrender them to the Lord. We believe that God is working on their hearts, and bringing other workers into their path that will minister to them, so that their wounds can heal, so that when they're ready, they can reach out to us and the relationship can be healed. As adults, they have to make their own decisions, and we have to respect their decisions."

In any family, the marriage always has to come before all other human relationships. Even before your children. It's the first priority of marriage, and a principle given to us by God. It's a tragedy when your children can't accept that truth, but it doesn't change the importance of standing true to God's principles.

"If you're ever stuck in a situation where you have an ultimatum," said Will, "where your child [says] it's either me or your spouse ... when you make that choice and stick with your spouse, they'll be mad. They'll be upset. And it could be for a long time ... But setting that example will have an impact on their lives. And [hopefully] there will be some sort of restoration."

When parents hold true to their Christian values and convictions, our kids are bound to notice. And we can only pray that they will eventually come around to embracing those principles in their own lives.

"God is all about redemption," Will added. "That's His story. On His business card is 'Redeemer.' Right now I need redemption in my life with my daughters. I need them redeemed. I need to reestablish that relationship."

If you've found yourself in that same situation, in need of redemption and restoration with your adult children, we encourage you to hold fast, and always do the right thing. Then trust God to honor your faithfulness and commitment.

God can do a miracle in any heart, no matter how wounded or hardened it might have become.

Chapter
thirteen

In-Home Dynamics

Traditional families have the luxury of starting out together, and getting used to each other as the family grows. They have a long history of navigating issues of personal space, sleeping arrangements, and family rules and traditions. The parents have usually established these things before they had kids, so everyone knows what to expect.

But all of these things become issues when you set out to blend two families into one. You are integrating kids who have never lived together, and parents who likely have different parenting styles and ideas about what family holidays and vacations should look like. Teenage boys suddenly have a roommate that they may not know very well, and girls have to suddenly share space in the bathroom with a new sister. And all the kids now have another parent telling them what to do.

Creating a sense of unity and family identity in this type of environment is often harder than it might appear. And usually more difficult than parents expect when they first decide to get married again.

It takes a level of intentionality to create a truly "blended" feel within a blended family, and our panel of successful stepfamilies had a lot of great ideas to draw from. Here are just a few of the strategies for success they shared with us:

Creating a Sense of Unity

"To create unity and identity for our family," said Renee, "the first thing we did was not to refer to our children as stepchildren, or his children and my children. We tried to always refer to them as 'our' children."

While it may be too early to expect your new stepchildren to call you 'Mom' or 'Dad,' it's never too soon to begin referring to them as your children. Introducing her son as your 'stepson' may be more accurate, but it's a term that may subtly feel like a disclaimer. Especially to kids who are already struggling to accept their new family. Not all kids will see it as an insult, but some might. So the best approach is to treat them as you would your own kids. It's important that your stepchildren see you treating them as your own, even if they don't initially reciprocate the sentiment.

Another important strategy for creating unity is to begin forming family traditions and activities. All of our successful stepfamilies agreed that this was perhaps the most effective approach to helping the family bond.

"We did family time together," said Renee. "We did game nights. We tried to create things that helped us interact on a friendlier, fun level. I think that's important for kids, especially."

Pete and Shana had a similar suggestion.

"How we created our new family identity," said Pete, "was to sit together as a family, pretty much for every meal—every dinner. And have conversations—open conversations. It created an atmosphere where everyone could share what they were feeling, you know, what their day was like. I think that helps."

We live in an era when life is so busy and fast-paced that family mealtime has largely become a thing of the past. But our couples agreed that having meals together is an important step to creating a strong sense of belonging and unity. It is a prime opportunity to get all of the family together at least once each day to just laugh and talk and enjoy being together. Having dinner in the den in front of the television may sound more relaxing, but it is a wasted opportunity for growth.

"One way that we created more unity was to have holidays at home," said Philip. "I was used to—as a single parent—going to my mother's house, or my father's house ... for Christmas and Thanksgiving. So when I first got married I wanted to do the same thing. But one of the things my wife stressed was, we need to start our own traditions. We need to have our own thing going on at our house so our kids can have memories of that. They can have memories of waking up on Christmas Day and leaving their bedroom and going to the Christmas tree and opening their presents at home."

It's almost impossible to overstate the value of fun holiday traditions when creating a strong family bond. This is true in any family, but exponentially important in a blended one. If kids see holidays come and go with little or no fanfare, they will begin to sense that doing fun things together is not that important to you. If you seem disengaged, they will disengage. Strong family traditions have the opposite effect. They create regular times of engagement for the family, and generate a sense of anticipation and excitement. Kids see holidays as something to look forward to, and a time to just enjoy being together and have fun as a family. Regular family traditions are a common trait of almost all healthy, happy families. Including blended families.

And when creating new family traditions, it's a good idea to let your children have input, and bring them into the process.

"I think as you're building a family," suggested Ty, "letting the children say, 'We would like to do this,' will help them feel included. It will help them feel like … we're building something together. Instead of the parent just saying, 'We're going to do this.' The 'pushing' feeling in a blended family can be all too common, so I think bringing the children in and saying, 'What do you think,' is a big part of them feeling [like] we're a family."

Whether planning family mealtimes, holiday traditions, family vacations, or just a special night out at the local skating rink, the key is to focus on what will make your children feel more bonded and unified. Getting families to blend takes intentionality and purpose. Special times together won't happen unless you work to create them.

Developing Personal Space

"In regard to personal space," confessed Charles, "when we first got married, it didn't go over so well. I immediately came in as the non-biological parent and established my domain. He [Ty's son] was used to it being his domain, and it caused a problem between us that affected the whole atmosphere of the house. It wasn't just an individual thing, but it was our entire home in an uproar."

Like a lot of new blended families, Charles and Ty had to learn how to integrate more gradually and deliberately. Though Ty's son was young, he still had a need to feel that his personal space and standing in the home was respected. It isn't easy having a new dad come into the house and begin to take charge. So Charles learned from his mistake, and when he and Ty began having children together, they set some clear boundaries and rules for the whole family.

In some blended families, there is also a matter of modesty that needs to be acknowledged and addressed. When stepsiblings of different genders move into the same household, creating clear boundaries and rules of personal space becomes even more critical.

You need to discuss things like appropriate dress around the house, keeping doors closed, and knocking before entering a room. Many of these issues of privacy are common sense, but don't assume that everyone will be on the same page. As parents, it's our job to communicate any rules and regulations we set for our household. This is a dynamic that Bryan and Velory had to navigate when they decided to get married.

"We have boys and we have girls,' said Velory, "so we did have to establish some boundaries there, and say, 'You have to be respectful, and you always knock before you go into anyone's door. You don't just go into anybody's room. You have to respect the girls' space, and girls, you have to respect the boys' space. If they have their door closed, you knock.' We had to establish that because the girls had always been with girls. I only have two girls, and they walked into each other's room whenever—they shared a room. With the boys it was the same thing. So … personal space and boundaries … we had to be intentional about that with the kids."

Pete and Shana had a different situation.

"We didn't have the room to put everybody in their own private location," explained Shana. "We had open discussions, like, 'Where would you feel comfortable sleeping?' Our two girls were fine in the king bed, but the boys said, 'We're not sleeping together.' So they got bunk beds … If you have that contention in their sleeping space and their private space, I think that can bleed over into other areas."

"That was very important to us … there was a lot of compromise but we were very open, and we were willing to hear everyone's feelings and thoughts on that. And we did the best we could with it."

In many blended families, children only come for weekends or during holidays, and those kids need personal space as well. Otherwise, time at your home will always feel awkward and uncomfortable.

This was a dynamic that Richard and Sheri had to deal with.

"We thought it was really important when the kids first started coming over," said Sheri, "for them to have their own personal space … I never wanted the kids to feel like they were weekend kids. I wanted them to know that both homes were home.

We had one extra bedroom and we got bunk beds. It was never awkward. They just came in, and soon as they got there … they knew they were home. You would never know that they didn't live in our house full-time."

And children aren't the only ones who need personal space. You and your spouse should discuss your own needs for privacy and respect—especially when one or both of you have been living on your own for several years.

"I think it is one of those things you should probably have a conversation about," said Bryan. "You know, 'What are some of the areas that you would prefer me not to mess with?' For some guys it's the garage. For some it's his corner of the living room, or maybe a little section in the bathroom. Go into the conversation with the attitude, 'It's not me against you, or you against me,' It's, 'How can I help us be together but still try to give you that space that's important to you?'"

"There are things that are important to me, and if I don't tell her what those are, I can't expect her to know it. I can't read her mind, and she can't read mine. It's another thing you need to be intentional about."

Living in harmony takes a lot of patience and communication, especially when trying to blend two previously independent families into one. There are no issues of space and privacy that can't be overcome with the right attitude of caring and cooperation. The important thing is to talk things through, and to show sensitivity to everyone involved. Because tension and resentment is the last thing you need when trying to bring a family together as one unit.

Shifting Authority to the Stepparent

When first starting out as a blended family, it's a good idea to let the biological parent be the primary disciplinarian of the children. This gives the stepparent time to relax and get to know his new kids on a more personal and friendly level. This is the approach that most successful stepfamilies took at the beginning, because it works.

It's a strategy that Moises and Maggie had to learn the hard way.

"I came in a little strong," confessed Moises, "and I realized that that wasn't getting me anywhere. They were so used to just getting the 'yes' or 'no' from Mommy. So as soon as I realized that, I started communicating with my wife. For parents coming into a relationship, I'd say, allow the kids to get used to you."

Children need to be eased into the idea of having a new parent in the house, so allowing the stepparent to take a back seat when it comes to discipline is a good idea—at least for the first few months.

But there comes a point when the stepparent's role should begin to shift and take hold, because homes only work when both parents share equal authority over the children. Otherwise the kids will begin seeing the stepparent as passive and disengaged.

In the case of younger children, that should be sooner, rather than later.

"One of the things that we did," said Philip, "was we sat down our son and told him, 'Hey, this is … your stepmother. She has the rights and privileges of a mother in this home, because this is her home as well … This is her home as much as it is our home. You need to understand and respect her authority.' That's one of those things where you want to set up the expectation … Sometimes you feel like you're inundating them with information, and you're telling them so much, but you want to get it out there."

That approach worked well with Philip and Valenceia because their son was relatively young when they married. But older children may need more time to get used to the idea.

That was the case with J.D. and Andi.

"In our situation, my oldest son had been the man of the house for a long time," explained Andi, "and he carried the weight of the world on his shoulders. So it was such a process for that weight to be taken off his shoulders, and for the man of the house to [become] the man of the house. To allow that to happen, as a mother, is really hard. For one thing, you're used to the way you interact with your children. There are a number of things that you have to be prepared to let go of. Let go of your sense of control. And let go of the need to always be in charge. And I think having a really good understanding of the man as the head of the household is going to do wonders for you as you step into that new role."

And once you've crossed that barrier and both assumed the roles of equal authority figures in the home, it's important to stay the course.

As Valenceia explained: "As a stepparent, you have to be consistent, because if you're not, they're not going to take you seriously, or give you that respect, because you're not taking yourself seriously. So you have to [show] a united front—when your spouse is there and when they're not there—you have to be consistent."

Households only run smoothly when both parents are unified in matters of discipline and house rules and expectations. And, when both parents share an equal role in establishing and administering those rules. That's true in every home, not just a blended one. Healthy rules make for healthy families.

When You Have Different Parenting Styles

"It's probably rare that blended family parenting styles, coming together, are going to match," J.D exlpained. "So it needs to be a compromise instead of the parents butting heads and the children trying to play them against one another. You have to be on the same page."

His wife Andi agreed with him. "The thing with parenting in a marriage [when] you've both come from previous marriages," she added, "[is] you have so much stuff that you have in your past. So much, 'I did this wrong.' And 'That person did that wrong.' There are just so many things that are factoring in. So you just constantly have to keep in communication with your spouse, and make sure you're not letting those things from your past creep in and interfere with your marriage—your family now."

Different parenting styles are inevitable any time you have a new blended family. The way we parent is usually established early in our marriages, so we are likely to have more in common with our first spouse when it comes to setting rules and doling out discipline. In second or third marriages, you have to rethink and reestablish those styles. Sometimes that takes a willingness to negotiate and compromise.

"We definitely had different parenting styles," said Renee. "And I think that part of how you work together in bringing those styles together is that you have to embrace the differences … If we can embrace the fact that God brought these two parenting styles together for a purpose, and work together, we can help balance each other out. I think that's key."

Richard and Sheri had many of the same challenges—and similar advice.

"She has a dictionary of how things were done in her family," said Richard, "and the way she's seen it done … and I have a dictionary of how things are supposed to be done … So when something comes up, she [says] 'In my dictionary it says this.' I look at my dictionary, and this is what it says. But you have to rewrite your dictionaries."

"You have to see what works for both of you. You might have done something different in your other marriage than you're doing now, but there's always room for growth. There's always room for improvement. These are the things that make or break marriages. She has to be able to come and tell me something that I'm doing wrong, or that could stand improvement. And I have to be able to take it, and not turn against it, and start to defend myself. I need to be able to take it in, listen to it, and make an improvement in our marriage."

A willingness to communicate and grow is one of the most critical aspects of a healthy marriage. And that same attitude is needed when trying to establish family rules and expectations. When parenting styles don't match, kids will soon become confused and frustrated. They need to see a unified front, and it's our job to come together in order to find that unity.

In addition to parents with different parenting styles, you also have children with different disciplining needs. It's important to find common ground on how to deal with that as well.

"Because of the different ages and the different backgrounds they were raised with," said Shana, "we have to use wisdom. You can't discipline them all the same. They all need consequences for actions … but it's not necessarily going to be the same with each child. I think you have to know that child's personality. You don't want to crush their spirit. And we want a positive result. We don't want them to do it again. So how do we get to that?"

The goal in discipline is to teach children the right and wrong ways to act, and it takes different methods for different children. As in all areas of training, that takes time, wisdom, and patience—and a willingness to get to know your children on an individual basis, in order to discover the best way to teach and motivate them.

So what happens when you disagree on how best to discipline?

"It's important to pray about it," said Bryan. "Pray together or pray separately before you have some of these conversations. You have to look at it from a respectful perspective."

Parents who pray together over family issues are always going to be better prepared to make wise decisions. And they will be in a better state of mind when they do so.

And when you have an issue or crisis that seems insurmountable, don't be afraid to seek help from a qualified pastor or counselor.

"Moral and parenting standards can break families," said Craig. "So I think that probably one of the most important things you can do is seek outside help—outside counsel—and discuss it. Because just between the two, there's going to be this butting of heads, whereas someone that you respect … can really draw this out to work it together."

In the words of the Proverbs writer, "Where there is no guidance the people fall. But in abundance of counselors there is victory."[17]

When blending two families into one healthy, united family, it's impossible to get too much godly advice and counsel.

Chapter fourteen

Extended Family Relationships

No matter how hard you work at creating peace and harmony within your own four walls, there are relationships outside your walls that have to be navigated just as carefully. In a blended family, you likely have a number of extended family members who want to play a part in your children's lives, and many of them deserve to do so.

Your ex-spouse wants to have some sort of relationship with the children you had together. They are still your children's parent, no matter how difficult or uncivil the divorce or breakup may have been. And your ex-in-laws often feel the same way. They still love and care for their grandkids, and are often struggling to figure out how they factor into your children's future.

Sometimes these relationships are healthy and good for your children. Sometimes they are not. In some cases, you feel the need to protect your kids from people who may harm them emotionally or spiritually.

It's a fine line that virtually every couple in a blended family has to deal with. And no two cases are the same. As parents, it's our job to understand all the dynamics at work in our particular family, and decide how to best handle all the outside factors and influences at work within our extended family relationships. Following is just a little hard-won advice and counsel from our panel of successful stepfamilies that may help:

Dealing With Ex-In-Laws

"We've had grandparents show up on Christmas Day unannounced with gifts … not calling, and just creating a ruckus," explained Ty. "So we really had to set boundaries."

Dealing with ex-in-laws may be one of the more common—and difficult—family dynamics facing most stepfamilies. Your spouse's parents didn't divorce you or your children, but at times they may feel like it.

They are usually walking on the same eggshells as you, and don't always handle it as tactfully or sensitively as you might hope. But they are usually doing the best they can in an awkward situation.

They want to have some kind of relationship with their grandchildren, but they have to go through you to do it. And you have to decide what that relationship should look like.

Many on our panel agreed that the key is open and honest dialogue, as well as healthy, well-defined boundaries.

"There needs to be some kind of communication," said Ty. "As a couple, you should come together and decide what's acceptable and what's not acceptable … It's hard, because these are grandparents, but you have to set the boundaries for your family, because you have to protect the children, you have to protect your spouse. For me, I was the one to do those things, because I was the one who was in the family."

When setting boundaries with ex-in-laws, or other extended family members, the focus should always be on what's best for the children. If their relationship with their grandparents is a healthy one—spiritually and emotionally—you likely want them to play a significant role in your children's future. But if it's not, your job is to protect your kids from undue harm. That's something only you and your spouse can decide. And then once you decide, to articulate your wishes as best as you can.

"Be willing to say … what your expectation is," said Renee, "what your need is, and hope they honor that. You can't make them honor it, but [you can] hope they are willing to work with you. And I think, when dealing with your ex-in-laws and your ex-spouse, be as kind as you can be, even when stating what you need, or what's expected. The more you can coat that in kindness, the more they will listen."

The most important aspect of setting clear and healthy boundaries is to not only articulate those boundaries, but to be diligent in enforcing them. And as always, couch your words in kindness and sensitivity.

"You don't want to have a situation where your kids don't have the opportunity to have a relationship with extended family," explained Craig. "That's very important … But you have to set boundaries. Not in the presence of the children. It's not their boundary to set; it's our boundary to set. So you have that … adult conversation with them. You say, 'We would love for you to have a relationship … so if you could think of something special that you guys would really like to do together, that would be great.' Turn it into an encouragement … Say, 'Look, I'd really like to figure out something that will work, and really make a great relationship.'"

In every situation, the best approach is always to be honest, but sensitive. To let your wishes be known, but also be willing to bend and be flexible. Your kids will benefit by getting to know their extended family members, and life will be less stressful if you don't feel the need to constantly be on your guard.

Dealing With an Absent Parent

Sometimes, protecting your children from overly involved family members is the least of your worries. There are cases when people who should be involved in your children's lives are nowhere to be found. And you have the job of explaining to your children why their dad or mom doesn't come to see them.

When an ex-spouse is distant or uninvolved, it can be devastating to your children. They may struggle to understand why their parent is absent.

"My ex was present at first," said Andi, "and now has vanished. We haven't heard from him in nearly two years. And he's dealing with some substance abuse issues. I tried to talk to the boys about it some. I don't want to constantly bring it up, but I want them to understand that their dad's issues are his issues, not theirs. They didn't cause it. They can't cure it."

J.D. and Andi found themselves in a common but uncomfortable situation. Andi's former husband was emotionally unhealthy, and had issues that made a healthy relationship impossible. So she had to explain to her children why their father was never around. Her primary concern was to make sure her boys didn't internalize their father's problems, or blame themselves for his absence.

It was a fine line to walk, and took an extra measure of love and sensitivity on her part. So she handled it the best she could. And she encouraged her sons to pray for their dad, and to try and understand the difficulties he was going through. "I think it's very important if there is an absent parent," explained Charles, "or a parent is in and out of the child's life, and there's inconsistency, that you do not allow the child to process that alone. You walk with them, with empathy, through the entire process. And let them ask whatever questions … because ultimately I believe you're teaching them how to relate to God in difficulty, and how to relate to God when things aren't happening according to what they feel should happen. So instead of trying to fix them, allow them to walk through the process."

Children aren't always capable of processing the pain and emotions they are experiencing on their own. As parents, it's our job to help them through any struggles or insecurities they may be having. The key is to know what damaging emotions our kids might be struggling with, and to recognize those times when they may need our help.

Charles and Ty worried about their son when his father wasn't around, especially during his early years. But with a lot of love and patience, they helped him navigate the feelings he was experiencing. And as their son got older, he learned to deal with it on his own.

"There's an interesting scenario we had this year," said Charles. "[Our son] got ahold of a resource called *Freedom From Your Past,* which is a Jimmy Evans book that we had around the house. And he said, 'I've forgiven my dad.' And we just kind of looked at each other and said, 'What do you mean?' He said, 'Well, I was reading in *Freedom From Your*

Past, and Jimmy gave me specific steps on forgiving my father. And he told me why forgiveness is essential, and how it will stunt my emotional and spiritual growth if I don't forgive him. I'm not a hundred percent there, but I've started blessing my father.'"

Children are much more resilient and understanding when they have a mature and godly parent to lean on in times of struggle. You may be the only healthy role model in your child's life, but if you stay close to them, and become the anchor they most need in difficult times, chances are good they will weather the storms and come out on the other side intact.

Healthy Boundaries With an Unhealthy Ex-Spouse

Dynamics change when you have an emotionally unhealthy spouse who not only wants to be involved in their child's life, but tends to be over-involved.

Because of joint custody agreements, parents often have a legal obligation to share their children with someone who is not a good influence on their lives. Your kids spend more time with your ex-spouse than you'd like, and you worry about the negative influences they may be absorbing.

Philip and Valenceia had joint custody of their son with his ex-wife, and they dealt with a lot of stress whenever he would spend time at her house. She would often undermine their household rules, and allow him to get away with things they didn't allow at home. So they had to work overtime at communicating their concerns, and trying to come to a healthy compromise.

"It may be uncomfortable," explained Philip. "It may be something that a lot of people don't want to do, but it's not about you. It's about the child … You want to make sure that you're having a conversation … We may not be at the best place relationship-wise, but we can all agree that we want the best for him … I think it's important to establish that. Whether they commit to it or not, it's important that you at least set that expectation. 'This is how we're going to run things over here. This is how we would hope that you do it over there. Because remember the goal. The goal is for him to succeed.'"

Craig and April had a similar situation. Their relationship with her ex-spouse wasn't a cordial one, but they were forced to communicate with him and his new wife regularly in order to work out the logistics of joint custody. Their advice was practical.

"We call meetings," said April. Any time a concern or issue would arise, she and Craig would address it head-on, no matter how uncomfortable it might be. And they made sure that both couples were present.

"I always make sure I'm there with my spouse when there's going to be a meeting," explained Craig.

Too often, couples allow frustrations and resentments to build and grow, simply because they don't want the uncomfortable task of talking to their ex-spouse about their concerns. But in this case, as in so many others, open communication is always the best approach.

"I had to be direct and blunt on the phone," explained Daniel, "and [stress that] this is about the child. It's not about emotions and feelings."

When it comes to our children, it's easy to allow tensions to run high and patience to run thin. But that's never the best way to handle an already uncomfortable situation. The key is to keep the focus on what's best for your children, and to continue reminding others to do the same.

Remember that children grow up, and there will be a time when issues of joint custody and shared living arrangements will no longer be a part of your life. But until then, face things head on, with patience, diligence, and a lot of prayer.

Chapter fifteen

Special Blended Family Challenges

When divorce involves children, there are usually financial ties to deal with as well as relational ones. And when it comes to money, things can easily get sticky and heated.

Most blended couples agree that life would be much easier if the courts were not so intimately involved in their lives or finances. But that's simply not the case for most stepfamilies, especially when the kids are young. Parents have an obligation to care for their kids, even after they divorce, and sometimes the State has to step in to make sure they do so. It's a necessity of life, but a breeding ground for conflict and resentment—especially among couples who are already struggling to get along.

Here are a few thoughts from our panel on handling some of the more common struggles which stepfamilies face when it comes to financial ties and obligations:

Child Support Challenges

"My ex-spouse kept taking me back to court for more child support," explained Will. "It's just one of those things where you have to go through it. Your children grow up eventually, and that child support does go away, but you've got to take care of your children. At the same time, hopefully you can have a relationship with your ex-spouse where you don't have that constant court battle going back and forth."

Not all ex-wives feel the need to punish their husbands on the heels of divorce, but that was often the case with Will's first wife. Their relationship was far from cordial, and she took her resentment out by dragging him back into court at every opportunity. Will and Wanda resented it, but there was little they could do. So they did their best to keep the relationship civil, even though it proved to be a financial strain on their family. They also had to deal with child support challenges from Wanda's

ex-husband. Except that he had a different attitude than Will. He resented the payments he had to make in order to support his kids, and often
looked for ways to get out of it.

"Child support was a huge source of fighting with my ex-husband
over the years," said Wanda. "It was always the threat of, 'I'm going to
take it away from you somehow. I'm either going to take our daughter
away from you so I don't have to pay child support … or I'll make sure
that I don't make any money so you don't get any child support.'"

Like a lot of ex-husbands, Wanda's ex resented the idea of having
to support children that weren't living under his roof, and he did all he
could to punish his ex-wife for expecting it of him. It eventually became
such an issue between them that Will and Wanda decided to do something about it. They determined that the little amount of money he gave
them wasn't worth the stress to their family.

"Finally, I made the decision to just release her dad of that obligation," explained Wanda. "I told him, 'You no longer need to pay me child
support.' I said, 'You do whatever you feel like you should do as a parent
to take care of her, whether you send money to me, or just take care of
things as you see needs arise…' So I freed him to be the parent that he
chose to be. And it freed me. It eliminated ninety-five percent of the
fighting we had going on between us."

Not all blended families would be in a financial position to do what
Will and Wanda did, but in their case it was the best approach. Since
child support was such a constant source of conflict, they decided to elim-
inate that struggle from their lives. And it proved to be a good decision.

In a perfect world, people would always take care of their financial
obligations, and voluntarily take care of their children. But we don't live
in a perfect world, so sometimes the best approach is to step up and be
the adult, even when others refuse to do so.

"You've really got to take into consideration the effect on the kids
anytime you go into court," said Scott, "regardless of their age."

"It isn't actually the money," Craig reminded us. "It's the emotional time you invest, where the focus should be on your marriage, on your children, and on your faith. These are the things we should be focused on."

How to Handle Lawsuits

One of the most frustrating by-products of divorce is that the courts suddenly become intimately involved in your affairs. And the more financial and relational ties you have, the more involved they seem to be.

It is never healthy or harmless for kids when their parents have to go to court on their behalf, but it's a necessary evil that many blended families have to deal with. People don't always own their responsibilities to their children, so the courts are often the only place to turn when dealing with problems of child support and shared custody.

"It's a sad situation," said Charles, "and it should be treated as such. It shouldn't be, 'Oh, we won.' Well, not really. It's about the child and you have to think about what's going on in the child's mind. So throughout the entire process, that's what was on our minds … Not to over-spiritualize it, but it took a lot of prayer to really understand and get the proper perspective on the situation."

Losing perspective is easy to do when negotiating on behalf of your children. But it's critical to keep reasonable expectations and a cool head, especially for the sake of your kids.

"I think it's easy to say, "Oh Lord, give us what we want,' and pray for what you really want to happen," Charles added. "but you have to understand, that's at the expense of someone else … So I think it should be treated with respect. I think it should be treated with care and understanding as to the entire situation."

"I would say to a parent who's going into a legal battle," said Ty, "to really lean on the Lord. Bring your spouse in and allow them to be a comfort to you. Be a team. Communicate what you think is best for the child."

When you're embroiled in a lawsuit, it's critical to keep the stress and turmoil from affecting your marriage and family. That's usually easier said than done, and takes a lot of prayer and spiritual guidance.

"I remember going through our lawsuit," said Will. " I never read the Bible so much in my life … We prayed about it. Our home group prayed about it … As stressful as it was, I feel like it brought us closer together … I think it has the potential to tear you apart, but for us it brought us closer together because we already had that foundation there."

It's impossible to go through a lawsuit without feeling some sort of stress on your marriage and family. No one gets through a legal battle completely unscathed. The key is to keep the strain from affecting your family any more than necessary, and that takes a great deal of patience and maturity. Our panel's advice was clear and unanimous. Lean on the Lord, and lean on each other, and trust God to get you through it intact.

Being Fair Financially With Stepchildren

Another financial issue that stepfamilies have to deal with is being fair and equitable with all of your children and stepchildren. Jealousy is already a common problem among stepsiblings, so it's important not to add to that tension. In any family, children are sensitive to issues of fairness and equality, but in blended families, kids tend to be even more tuned into it. When one child feels that another is being favored, it can create a lot of resentment and anger.

As parents, it's our job to make sure our children all feel valued and treasured—with our words, actions, and pocket books.

Richard and Sheri both brought children into their marriage, so issues of equity were important to them from the start. Not just financially, but emotionally.

"It's not about making it to where it has to be exactly equal," explained Sheri. "It's important to us that this is 'our' family, 'our' kids. They're not your kids or my kids, they're our children, and that's how we treat it—as if we gave birth to all of them and as if we've always been together."

Stepchildren are often hypersensitive to issues of fairness, but it can feel exhausting to have to keep track of every dime you spend on every child in order to make sure you're being completely fair. Kids have different needs, and some will inevitably cost more than others. What's important is to make sure they understand their value in the family, and that all of their needs are being met—physically, emotionally, and financially.

"If you're breaking this down into making sure that everything is equal," said Craig, "that everything is right, you're never going to win … The gift of gratefulness—that's what you really want to give them."

Our panel also agreed that fairness extends beyond your children's present needs. It's also important to think ahead into the future, and make sure all of your kids are taken care of after you're gone.

"I do think it's important as a blended family, that we have a will," said Jesi. "It's very complicated [what] happens if you die and there's no will in a blended family. I think it's important that you have that [regarding] any major assets that you have—that you would want to share that equally between your family."

Having a well-organized will is important in any family, but especially important in a blended one. If you don't, you could be setting your family up for a lot of resentment and hurt feelings in the event of your untimely death.

Family Traditions and Holidays

"One of the things we discovered early on," said Jesi, "as we blended our family, is that all the traditions that we had pretty much went out the door. They just were gone. And so what we began to do is find ways to create those new traditions."

Family traditions are important to children, and great ways for parents to create a sense of unity and belonging within the family. But in blended families, you often have competing expectations regarding family traditions and customs. One set of children may be used to celebrating Christmas at home, while the other set always went to Grandma's for the holidays. His kids may expect turkey and dressing for Thanksgiving dinner, while hers always looked forward to Italian food.

Blending these family traditions together to make everyone happy isn't always easy, and often the best approach is to start fresh, and create new family customs.

"I think it's okay in a blended family to make your own traditions," explained Sheri, "to come up with a new way of doing things. It's your family. You guys have to make it work... We just said, 'We are going to do things our way. We're going to try some new things.'"

Richard and Sheri had the same approach.

"I think that when you start to do your own traditions," said Richard, "and start doing different things than you did in your past relationship, it gives the kids a new life, and a new way of looking at things."

Blending family traditions takes a lot of compromise and creativity. You have to be willing to think outside the box, and then convince your children to do the same.

"Compromise is just huge in marriage," explained Richard, "but in a blended family, you have to have double compromise. I mean, you have to compromise about everything. But our nature is to want it the way we want it, so it's really hard sometimes to compromise, because we feel that our way is the right way. You know, 'Why should I have to compromise when this is the way we've always done it?'"

Craig and April agreed.

"Compromise is extremely important," said April, "because sometimes, with different situations going on, you may need to do something different that year than what you've always done. Especially when the children are a little bit older ... It really is important to listen to what they're wanting. You know, you just have to take a step back and say, 'I'm going to let you do that because I love you and want what's best for you.'"

"Blending is compromising," added Craig. "Blending is adapting to different situations, and they change all the time."

This was one point on which all of our successful stepfamilies seemed to agree. When it comes to bringing two families together under one roof, everyone has to be willing to give on some level and compromise for the good of the family.

"With compromise, you have to remember it doesn't just affect holidays," said Jesi. "It can affect sports, events at school ... it might be your weekend that there's a party at somebody's house that they just have to go to. It could be a tournament that you can't manage, but maybe your ex can ... Having that compromise, and being able to work through that as kids grow up is really important."

Dealing With an Empty Nest

In every family, there comes a time when children leave home and couples are left alone to navigate their relationship as a married couple. In blended marriages, however, it may be the first time since the couple met that they are able to relate to each other as just husband and wife, with no children in the picture. The kids have been a part of their marriage since the beginning, and that is the only reality they have ever known as a couple.

This doesn't sound like a huge problem, but for couples in blended families, it can be something of a shock to the system. They've been parents for so long, and have spent so much time and energy learning to blend, that they never really had the luxury of just focusing entirely on each other.

In these cases, couples often have to learn completely new skills and thought processes in order to stay connected.

"The key to success in empty nesting," said Monte, "and the empty nest time, is to really remember the reason why you fell in love in the first place. There are stresses with the kids, and stresses with family members, and maybe you're getting older, so there are other responsibilities to go with that. But you have to be a team."

In any marriage, the key to staying in love for a lifetime is focusing on each other's needs above all other human relationships. But blended family couples sometimes forget to do that. Then when the kids leave home, they have to learn to lean on each other. Otherwise the marriage is bound
to suffer.

"When you face all of these challenges," said Cliff, "you have to face it with the understanding that this partner of mine, and this life we share together is more vital and more important than any challenge we face."

Keeping the marriage your first and highest priority is critical in every stage of the relationship. But it becomes essential when the nest is suddenly empty and the two of you are left all alone.

The empty nest years can be the most exciting time of your marriage. But it can also be a frightening thought if couples have thrown all their energies into raising kids, and neglected their marriage in the process.

Don't let that be the case in your marriage. Whether blended or not, your spouse should be the most important person in your world, and nothing but your relationship with God should take a higher priority. Keep that at the forefront of your heart and mind, and do whatever it takes to keep your marriage healthy and growing.

If you do, your empty nest years will feel anything but empty.

Chapter
Sixteen

Widowed and Blended

Remarriage under any circumstance can be challenging, but when the death of a spouse is involved, it can take on an even greater level of trial and struggle.

Many may think that marrying a widow or widower would be easier than having an ex-spouse still in the picture, but there are issues at work that aren't always apparent on the surface. And when kids are involved, those issues can be overwhelming.

This dynamic only affects a small percentage of blended families, and if it doesn't pertain to your situation, you may want to skip ahead to the next chapter. But for those who have found themselves widowed and blended, we made a point of interviewing several couples who are successfully navigating those waters in order to get their thoughts and advice.

The challenges that widowed spouses bring to marriage are not always obvious, but they are most definitely there. And the children are affected just as deeply, even if they appear to be fine. It takes a special measure of patience and sensitivity to work through them.

Lingering Grief

"With the loss of a spouse, there's more anxiety and grief than one realizes," explained Monte. "There's a residual impact … that you don't always fully realize... In our relationship, as we were married, sometimes that would exhibit itself over time. And we had to adjust to that."

Monte was a widower when he met and married Kathleen. And he had many fond memories of his first wife. Unlike many divorced couples, Monte had nothing but good to say about his deceased wife, and his first marriage was a strong and healthy one. His kids also had fond memories of their mother when Kathleen came into the picture.

"The compounding element was with the children," said Monte, "because they had issues of their own to deal with... I had to be cognizant of those things. They want to be faithful to their mom. They don't want to dishonor their mom, and so [I had] to realize that they have an allegiance to their mom. And that's okay."

Both Monte and his children still missed his first wife, and although they grieved hard when she died, grieving never completely goes away. Kathleen understood this truth, and worked hard at giving them room to mourn her loss—even years later. She learned to recognize the stages of grief in order to better understand what they were going through. But it wasn't always easy.

"I knew about [his wife]," said Kathleen, "and as things would get heightened, or disgruntled, she became a saint. And so I felt like I was competing with a saint, because as time grew, she got nicer and nicer and nicer … I dealt with a lot of jealousy. It really is hard to compete with a dead person."

One of the most difficult aspects of being married to a widow or widower, is that the ex-spouse never quite goes away. They are always lingering somewhere in the memories of those they left behind. The key is to understand that your marriage is not a competition. And that just because your husband or wife is grieving a previous spouse, doesn't mean they love you any less. Your relationship is a separate entity, not an extension of their first marriage.

Give your family room to grieve, and don't begrudge them the memories they share of their former spouse and mother. Being angry or resentful will only cause more stress and tension.

Treat Memories With Respect

"I think when one spouse has passed away and you're now in a remarriage," said Katherine, "it's important to honor that spouse."

Katherine's husband Cliff was a widower when the two married, and he, too, had fond memories of his deceased wife. And his children grieved deeply when their mother died. Even after their father remarried, the kids hung tightly onto their mother's memory. Cliff's son hung a picture of his mother in his room, and often treated it as a shrine.

Katherine could have been jealous, but she instead chose to treat the situation with kindness and understanding. She knew she could never compete with her memory, so she didn't try. She instead worked to preserve her memory, and treat it with the utmost respect and honor.

"It's healthy for him," she said. "And it's healthy for [my girls]. Let's celebrate what's positive about people, no matter how [the marriage] ended."

Living in denial of grief and loss doesn't make it disappear. If anything, it just prolongs the grieving process. Getting over the loss of a parent can take years, even decades, and trying to hurry the process along can only make things worse.

A healthier approach is to encourage grieving children to talk about what they are feeling, and to help them articulate their sense of loss. In younger kids, this is especially important, even though it may be difficult for them. You might ask them to draw pictures of the special memories they have with their mother, and then talk about what they miss most about her. Then hang those pictures in their room.

It's a simple idea, but a good way to show children that you're not there to erase their mother's memory, or to try and take her place. You want to help them preserve and honor it. In doing so, you are helping them grieve in a healthy and honoring way—and in their own time.

Give Them Time to Grieve

Katherine married Cliff knowing that he still had feelings for his deceased wife, and that could have been a formula for disaster. Kathleen took that same chance when she married Monte. But both Katherine and

Kathleen understood some important truths about building a successful marriage with a widow or widower—truths that should be shared and understood by anyone who finds themselves in a similar situation.

First and foremost, they understood that it is possible for grief and love to co-exist. That even though your spouse's grief is real, so is their love for you and your family. Your marriage is not a competition. If you see it as one, you'll find yourself struggling with feelings of resentment and insecurity. The only healthy approach is to accept your spouse's grief, and be the one person in their life they can depend on as they work their way through it.

Second, they understood that grief takes time. And that rushing it is counter-productive. Mourning a loss is not the same as dwelling on the past. It's an important step in the grieving process, and needs to be accepted—and expected. When you marry a widow or widower, there will be times when episodes of grief and depression come their way. And as the loving, caring spouse, it's your job to give them time and space to get through it.

Finally, they understood that even as memories begin to fade, sparks of grief will always be present. A widowed person's grief is never fully pro-cessed, no matter how many years it has been since they lost their spouse. In time, the pain will soften, but their first spouse will always share a small piece of their heart.

That doesn't mean they love you any less. It's just a sign of your spouse's great capacity for love.

And isn't that why you married them in the first place?

Section Threee

Fundamentals of a Strong Family

Chapter
seventeen

Strong Families Begin With Strong Marriages

This has been a year of transition for our (Frank's) family. A year ago this month, our twenty-five-year-old son moved to Kansas City to work with a non-profit ministry. It was hard to see him go, but exciting to see him striking out on his own and following God's call for his life.

A few months ago, our twenty-two-year-old daughter got married to a wonderful, godly young man. It was a surreal day for my wife and I, and a joyous occasion for our family. She found an amazing husband, and for that we are infinitely grateful.

Today my wife and I are officially empty nesters. It's been an interesting period of change for us, and seemed to sneak up on us much faster than we expected. But we're thrilled to see what God has in store for us during this exciting new season of our marriage.

Now that the house is empty, I can see that this could have been a terrifying time of transition for us. The week after our daughter's wedding was likely the quietest week our home has seen in over a quarter century. For the past twenty-five years, kids have been constantly coming and going, bringing all manner of noise and chaos. Our home has been the epicenter of more parties and pizza nights and sleepovers than I could possibly keep track of.

And now, everything is still and quiet. Even our dog passed away this year, so it's just Ruthie and me, and a lot of silence. It's a good thing we're still crazy about each other, otherwise, we'd be in a world of hurt right now.

The Empty Nest Years

All marriages go through times of transition, but nothing quite as shocking to the system as when the kids leave home. The empty nest syndrome is a very real thing, and tends to catch a lot of couples by surprise. It's a time when a lot of marriages start to fall apart, simply because couples are unprepared for life after children.

Many marriages go through their toughest times of struggle and conflict during the empty nest years. In fact, today, the divorce rate among older, more established couples is growing in record numbers. Some studies suggest that the number of divorces among empty nesters has grown by sixteen percent since 1990.

Part of the cause can be traced to the number of baby boomers reaching their 50's and 60's over the last few decades, but that's not the only reason. I'm convinced that the primary cause is that couples tend to spend so much time and energy on raising children that they completely lose touch with each other. Then once the kids leave home, they feel lonely, disconnected, and out of love.

Attorneys call these late-life breakups "High Asset Divorces," because couples in this stage of life usually have a lot of financial ties to sort through. It's a booming industry among divorce lawyers, but I actually consider it one of the greatest of human tragedies, because it's not supposed to be that way.

The empty nest years are intended to be the most exciting years of marriage. They should be a time of joy and celebration. A time of looking back over the years of hard work, sleepless nights, and personal sacrifice in order keep your family on track and rejoicing over a job well done. It should be a time of reconnecting with each other as you look forward to an exciting new season of grandkids, extended vacations, and preparing for retirement. These are supposed to be the "Golden Years," where you get to relax and enjoy the fruits of your labor.

An empty nest should be filled with feelings of happiness and anticipation, not thoughts of regret and emotional detachment.

But for that to happen, you have to make a conscious effort to keep the marriage as your highest human priority. Everything else has to take a back seat, including your children.

The First Rule of Marriage

The greatest mistake many couples make is putting too much emphasis on raising children, and not enough energy on each other. Kids should not be the highest priority in your family. Your highest priority is to the marriage. Only your relationship with God should take a greater precedent.

I (Jimmy) often make that statement from the podium when I'm speaking on marriage issues, and I can always feel the pushback from a large number of parents in the audience. I can see the ones who don't agree with me by the look on their faces. Often it's the women who shake their heads and begin to whisper to their husbands. I can immediately tell that I've touched a nerve.

We've been conditioned to think that once you have kids, everything else takes a back seat—including your relationship with each other. Kids quickly become the number one priority in the family. Their needs and desires trump everything. Many couples allow their entire lives to revolve around the children, and they become addicted to keeping their kids happy and well-tended. They make endless sacrifices to indulge the children's every whim.

But that's a mistake. It's not healthy for kids to think that they are the center of the universe, and that their wants trump everything else. Kids who are raised believing that they are the most important things in the world do not grow up happy and well-adjusted. Often they become needy and narcissistic. Show me a brat and I'll show you a kid who has been doted on every minute by well-meaning parents.

Child-centered families don't raise secure children, because their priorities are usually out of balance. The healthiest kids come from families where the parents put the marriage relationship first. They love their children unconditionally, and are completely dialed in to their kids' most critical needs—physically, emotionally, and spiritually—but they don't allow the kids to become their highest human priority. The marriage is their most important relationship in the family.

The first rule of marriage, is that the marriage always comes first.

Always!

Keeping Marriage Your Top Priority

When our kids were young, Karen and I (Jimmy) had a lot on our plates, and our lives were extremely busy. As Senior Pastor of Trinity Fellowship in Amarillo, Texas, I had a lot of demands on my time and energy. And when the Lord called us to start our *Marriage Today* ministry, it took an even greater toll on our time. But we committed to never allowing our marriage and family to take a back seat to the needs of our church and ministry. We knew that if we kept our priorities in the right order, God would take care
of the physical and financial needs of both our church and our fledgling ministry to marriages.

Our relationship with God was always our highest priority, but after that, our number one priority was always our relationship with each other. Our kids came next, and everything else after that.

Dinnertime in our home was always our most guarded time together. Even when the kids were little, we made sure we all ate dinner together, then afterward we'd spend time in the family room, rolling on the floor and loving on the kids before bedtime. Around eight o'clock each evening, it was my job to tuck the kids into bed. So I'd get them dressed for bed and then read some verses from the Bible to help them unwind. I'd grab my guitar and lead them in a few worship songs, then pray with them before tucking them in for the night.

The kids knew that once they were in bed, they were not allowed to get up. They could read in bed for as long as they wanted, but they had to stay in their rooms. We told them, "This is mommy and daddy's time," and they knew we meant it. Then we would retreat to our bedroom and spend time talking and decompressing from the day. It was our time to connect with each other, one on one, and we guarded it carefully.

We also had a regular date night one evening a week, and we made sure it happened, no matter how busy life became. We would leave the kids with a babysitter that we trusted and then go out for the evening. Our kids knew that this was a non-negotiable part of our schedule.

Every couple of months we would leave our kids with their grandparents and go away for the weekend. We didn't have a lot of money back then, but we could always find a good deal on a hotel room, and we'd spend the entire weekend together with no distractions. This was our time to sow into each other, and reconnect.

Our kids grew up knowing that they were loved deeply, and that we would do anything for them, but our first priority was to each other. And because of it, our kids always felt secure, protected, and confident. There was never a hint of jealousy or resentment on their parts. It just felt natural and right to them.

Not only were we able to stay connected with each other, but we were setting an example for our kids that carried over into their own marriages. Today both of our children are married with kids of their own, and they both have stellar marriages. Their kids are extremely happy and well-adjusted, because their parents understand the first rule of marriage. Our kids learned from our example that the key to growing a healthy home is to always keep the marriage first.

A Healthy Legacy

That principle is true whether you are on your first, second, or tenth marriage. If you want this marriage to be your last marriage, make sure that your relationship to each other is always your most important human relationship. If you do that, the empty nest years will be the happiest, most rewarding years of your life. You'll thank God you didn't lose touch with each other during the busyness of work and kids and the many other obligations of life.

Your kids will thank you. And they'll be glad that they have happy and healthy grandparents to babysit their kids when they want to work on building their own strong marriages.

As a husband, the greatest thing you can do for your children is to love their mother, and to cherish her the way she longs to be cherished.

As a wife, the greatest thing you can do for your children is to love their father. To give him the respect and admiration he needs, and never lose sight of your most critical human relationship.

But don't allow them to become the center of your family's universe. That spot should always be reserved for your spouse. The example you set now will ring through your family for generations to come.

Chapter eighteen

Strong Families Have Right Priorities

Before I (Jimmy) was a pastor and a speaker, I was an appliance salesman. And I was good at it. My first month on the job I outsold every other salesman on the floor, and I continued to be the top seller month after month. In fact, I sold so much that my boss came to me one day and said he was restructuring my commission agreement.

When I asked him why, he said, "If I paid you what I promised, you'd be making more than my top salesman, and I couldn't do that to him."

I sat in his office thinking, "I thought I was your top salesman?" But I needed the job, so I had the good sense not to argue with him.

At the time, Karen and I were heavily involved in our church family at Trinity Fellowship in Amarillo, Texas. We had life group meetings several evenings a week, and I taught Bible class every Sunday morning. We were an integral part of the church, and loved being involved in a lot of church programs and ministries.

One day a man I had met at the appliance store came to my house to offer me a sales job. He was a wealthy businessman in Amarillo, and the job he offered would have been much more lucrative than the one I had. I could have doubled my salary, and had more room for promotions and benefits.

I was getting excited about the prospect until he mentioned that I would have to work evenings and weekends. I said to him, "I'm sorry, but I already have a lot of commitments to my life groups during the evening hours, and Sunday morning church is important to us. I'd love to work for you, but I can't work on evenings or weekends."

He almost acted offended when I told him that. He stiffened his back and said, "Are you serious? You're going to turn down the best job of your career because of church?" He literally laughed at me, right there in my living room. I told him again, "I'm sorry, but I'm not willing to give up my commitments to my church family. I guess you'll just have to find someone else."

It was a tough job to turn down, because we really could have used the money at the time. But I knew it would be wrong to put money above my commitments at church. I also didn't want to set a bad example for my children. So I turned down the offer, and stayed at the appliance store.

It turned out to be one of the best decisions I have ever made, because several years later, I was asked to come on staff at Trinity Fellowship. Soon afterward, I was hired as the Senior Pastor, and today I still serve there as a Pastor and Elder. Trinity has been our family for over thirty years, and I thank God every day that I didn't throw all that away for a few extra dollars of income.

I made the right decision, and God has blessed our family for it ten times over.

The Quest For Success

There are no greater blessings in life than the blessings that God has in store for those who love Him and keep His commandments. And the fastest way to activate those blessings and open the floodgates of heaven, is to live your life with right priorities. God longs to shower His people with good gifts and a blessed life, but He can only do that when we stay in His will and seek out His desire for our lives.

Too often in our quest for success we focus on worldly treasures and the approval of men, and in the process, we completely miss what God has in store for our future. Our priorities get skewed because we are chasing after blessings that are as fleeting as they are meaningless.

The world has a shallow and distorted definition of success. And the way we measure it is not always the way God would measure it. I've noticed at least seven different measures of success that most people strive to attain:

1) *Financial prosperity.* Having money is the primary way most people define success, simply because money is so important to our daily lives. It's something we all need in order to get by. And the more you have, the more successful you feel. People who have money are seen as the "movers and shakers" of society. They have more things, more freedom, more status, and more value in the eyes of the world.

For many, financial prosperity is the only measure of success. It's all they really strive for because they think it will bring them all the happiness and contentment they need.

2) *Popularity.* On some level, we all long to be popular and attractive. We want others to like us, so we strive for fame and recognition. Attractive people usually have more friends, and are held in high esteem, so we strive to be handsome or good-looking. There is no industry on the planet that brings in more money than the beauty industry, because in today's society, looks are everything. Many people spend their entire lives seeking after fame and beauty and notoriety. They sell their souls in order to be popular.

3) *Power and influence.* Many people measure success by the amount of authority and power they have over others. Often those who gravitate toward politics or leadership positions are driven by a need to be respected. When we hold positions of authority, it gives us a sense of accomplishment and value. Power can be an intoxicating drug, and can easily cause people to lose perspective and compromise their principles. People with narcissistic tendencies often define success by the amount of authority and influence they have over others.

4) Relationships. Some people gauge success by the number of friends they have, and the strength of their relationships. They would rather love and be loved than to have money or power or influence. This actually is not a bad measure of success, since God also puts a lot of stock in relationships. But friends alone won't make us happy. And sometimes, people who long for relationships are driven more by co-dependence than spiritual values.

5) Education and intellect. There is a segment of society that values education and IQ above all other endeavors. They define success by the number of diplomas a person has, or the educational accolades they happen to attain. They place the highest priority on intellectual achievements, and often measure their worth by their ability to out-think or out-debate others. These types of people often gravitate toward careers in science or education. And they can easily become intellectual snobs and elitists, looking down on those who are less educated.

6) Giftedness. Many people who are artistically gifted measure success according to creative achievement. They are most moved by music or art or fashion, so that becomes their measure of accomplishment. Musicians might measure success by their ability to score an elaborate piece of music, or play a beautiful composition. An artist might measure success by how well they can paint a striking landscape. A photographer might be motivated by their ability to capture the perfect sunset or facial expression. Gifted athletes may be motivated by achievements on the playing field. Many people are driven by the need to hone their gifts and talents, and that becomes their primary measure of personal success.

7) Security. Some people define success by personal security—either physical or financial. They have a need to feel safe and protected if things go wrong, so they put their emphasis on being secure. They may have a large nest egg saved up for the future, and the more they have, the more successful they feel. Other people find security in being able to protect themselves physically. They may invest their time in learning self-defense, or become adept at handling firearms. Success is measured in their ability to ward off attackers, or weather a physical or financial catastrophe.

God's Definition of Success

There is nothing inherently wrong with any of these endeavors. Each of these seven measures of accomplishment is worthy of our time and effort when kept in the right perspective. Money can be a good thing in the right hands, and God often rewards people with financial success when they tend their money well. God also gives people influence and authority when they have proven worthy of it. Relationships are critical to all of us, and education is a great way to better ourselves. All gifts come from God, and He wants us to use our gifts for His glory. And there is nothing wrong with being diligent and pragmatic. Security is a good thing when kept in perspective.

The trouble comes when these things become the measure of our worth in the world. When we define success by worldly values, we are destined to fail, because the world is evil and fallen. And the world's priorities are not God's priorities.

God measures success in terms of spiritual values and commitment. He cares most about our relationships with Him and with others.

When the Pharisees asked Jesus about the greatest commandment, he replied, "Love the Lord your God with all your heart and with all your soul and with all your mind.' This is the first and greatest commandment. And the second is like it: 'Love your neighbor as yourself.' All the Law and the Prophets hang on these two commandments."[18]

Jesus' definition of success is simple and straightforward. Loving God is our first and greatest priority, and loving others is next in line.

God considers us successful in life when we spend our time and effort on spiritual relationships and values. In God's economy, it is love and obedience that trumps all other human endeavors.

These are the right priorities that we should focus on as followers of Christ. And this is the definition of success that should drive everything we say and do within our families. It is what we need to teach and model for our children, and the first question we should ask ourselves in any given decision or situation.

Living With Right Priorities

The biggest problem with living by the world's definition of success is that it skews one's view of reality. A person can attain every standard of achievement he sets for himself, yet still be a failure in God's eyes. He can be rich and famous beyond his wildest dreams, have power and influence over others, have more relationships than he can manage, be educated and gifted and secure, yet still have none of the spiritual qualities that God longs for him to have.

In the same way, a person can appear to be an utter failure at life yet infinitely successful in the eyes of God. By the world's standards, he may achieve nothing, yet God sees him in a different light. By God's standards, he is a spiritual giant!

And it is right priorities that make all the difference.

By the world's definition of success, Jesus himself was a failure. He had almost none of the qualities that society looks for when gauging personal achievement. He died penniless, with only a handful of friends in His corner. He was so unpopular that they hung Him on a cross.

The prophet Isaiah wrote, "He had no beauty or majesty to attract us to Him, nothing in His appearance that we should desire Him. He was despised and rejected by mankind, a man of suffering, and familiar with pain. Like one from whom people hide their faces He was despised, and we held Him in low esteem."[19]

In the eyes of the world, Jesus was a complete failure at life. But you and I know differently. Jesus was the most successful man to ever walk the earth. In God's eyes, there has never been His equal. No person has ever had a greater eternal impact on the world. He is the greatest man to ever live, and His story is the greatest story ever told.

Jesus is the standard by which every believer strives to live.

This is the definition of success that God holds dear. And it is the standard of achievement that you and I most need to pass onto our children.

Strong families are built on right priorities. And right priorities begin and end with the person of Jesus.

A Dose of Perspective

Many years ago, I (Frank) wrote an article for a Christian periodical called *Discipleship Journal*. It was one of my first published articles, so it was an exciting accomplishment for me. The article was on the topic of materialism, and the need for Christians to throw off the obsession with earthly possessions and instead focus on heavenly treasures.

I still remember getting my first copy in the mail. My wife and I sat on the floor of the living room to admire the layout and artwork, and to read it all the way through. The editor had done a great deal of trimming, so the word count was only about half of what I originally submitted, but it was still exciting.

Since magazine writers get paid by the word, I found myself counting the words one by one, just to see how much I would be making for the piece. Somehow the irony of that was completely lost on me at the time. Here I had published an article on the evils of greed, yet found myself obsessed with how much I would be paid for the article.

I'd say that's a good example of wrong priorities.

That very evening during dinner we got a phone call from an area code in New York. It was a young man who asked if I was the Frank Martin who had written the article in the most recent issue of *Discipleship Journal*. I told him I was, and he was happy to have finally located me. He had apparently just read the article, and wanted me to know what a powerful impact it had on him.

"I've been climbing the corporate ladder for as long as I can remember," he told me, "and I've reached every goal I've ever set for myself. I've been extremely successful in my career. Yet I've never been happy. No matter how much I make, it still feels empty."

He went on to explain that he had just made an offer on an expensive condominium in Manhattan, and was scheduled to sign the paperwork that afternoon. Until his copy of *Discipleship Journal* arrived in the mail. My article was the first one he read, and God used it to bring a wave of conviction to his heart and spirit.

"I've decided not to buy the condominium," he told me. "And I promised God that I'm going to completely change my priorities. I felt called to the ministry in high school, but I've never been obedient to that calling. I told God today that I'm going to stay in my apartment and enroll in Bible Seminary. I think God wants me to be a preacher, so that's what I'm going to do."

I was literally shaking and in tears as I hung up the phone that evening. I still couldn't quite process the conversation. The idea that something I had written could have had such a profound impact on someone I had never met was an unbelievable blessing to me, and I praised God for bringing these words of encouragement my way.

I also felt a deep conviction in my spirit for my attitude earlier that day. And I prayed a silent prayer of repentance. It was an experience I've never forgotten, and it brought a level of perspective that only God can bring.

God loves us deeply, but He resists the wrong priorities that seep into our hearts when we buy into the world's view of success. Because wrong priorities give Satan a foothold in our lives that keeps us from finding the blessings that God so longs to give.

The greatest thing you can do for your family is to guard your priorities with a vengeance. Keep them right and righteous and godly. Make your priorities God's priorities. And teach your children to do the same.

If you do that, you may never reach the world's standard of success, but in the eyes of God, you will always be a rock star!

Chapter *nineteen*

Strong Families Are United

In high school, I (Frank) played second trumpet in the school band, and I also played in the Concert Orchestra. I wasn't very good, but it was an easy A. Every day the director would begin class by rapping his baton on the podium to signal the beginning of class.

We would all immediately get quiet, then he would point to the girl who played the Oboe. She would raise her instrument to play the note of "A," just above middle "C." The director called this note "Concert A," and it was the note we used to pitch the entire orchestra. We would all listen carefully, because that was our signal to tune our instruments to that specific note.

We only had a few seconds to do it, so we had to be quick. Then once the conductor thought we were ready, he would raise his baton high in the air, and once again there was silence. It was time to begin the first piece.

Without this ritual, I can't imagine what our orchestra might have sounded like. We'd never have been able to get through a sheet of music, because we'd all have been in a different key. "Concert A" was the note that kept everything working together. It brought order out of chaos. It brought clarity out of confusion. It brought the entire orchestra in sync, allowing us to sound like we actually knew what we were doing.

Without it, we'd have sounded more like a bag of angry cats than an award winning concert orchestra.

Every orchestra practices this ritual, because without everyone tuned to "Concert A," they'd never be able to create beautiful music.

Finding "Concert A"

That same dynamic is true when it comes to families. All families need a "Concert A" to keep them together and on track. In a family, there has to be a strong sense of unity, agreement, and hierarchy. You need parents who are united in their vision for the family, and kids who understand that the parents are in charge.

In blended families, there can't be a sense of "his" kids, and "her" kids. There can be no favorites among parents or siblings. Both parents have to have equal say and authority over the children, and they have to be in agreement with each other. Everyone has to work together.

Harmony only happens when families are in sync and tuned to the same pitch and tempo. This is the "Concert A" of healthy and successful families. And it is a universal truth, regardless of the family dynamics, whether it is a traditional family or a blended one.

Without "Concert A," there is chaos and confusion and rebellion.

I (Jimmy) have a friend who married a divorced woman with teenage children, and the woman's son was not happy about the relationship. He was still upset about his parents' divorce, and always held out hope that they would get back together again, even though the relationship was a highly dysfunctional one.

The boy let his mother know that he would never accept her new marriage. He didn't accept the relationship before the wedding, and he had no intention of changing his mind afterward.

During the wedding reception, he took his new stepfather aside and said to him, "I just want you to know that I plan to make your life miserable. Starting tomorrow, I'm going to be your worst nightmare!"

And that's exactly what he did. No matter how hard my friend tried to get close to his new stepson, the boy refused to accept him. His new stepson did all he could to undermine the relationship and cause disunity among his parents. He ignored the family rules, and acted out at every opportunity. And it made life miserable for everyone—especially his mother.

I felt sorry for them, because without this boy's cooperation, the family was in a constant state of conflict and struggle. His attitude affected every aspect of their relationship. It set a bad example for the younger siblings, and they began acting out as well.

They couldn't even have a peaceful meal together, because this one member of the family refused to let it happen. He was determined to stay out of sync with the rest of the family.

Everyone in the orchestra was in tune, except this one lone instrument. He refused to tune to "Concert A," and because of it, the entire orchestra was in constant chaos and confusion.

A Biblical Command

The Bible has a lot to say about the importance of unity within a family. Paul wrote to the Ephesians, "Children, obey your parents in the Lord, for this is right. 'Honor your father and mother...so that it may go well with you and that you may enjoy long life on the earth.'"[20]

Children are commanded to submit to their parents, and to obey their rules and instructions. When kids are disobedient and disruptive, it not only creates havoc in the family, but grieves the Lord. God promises blessings on children who obey this commandment, because in God's eyes, submission to authority is critical to growing and maintaining a strong family unit.

Paul goes on in this same letter to speak to fathers: "Fathers, do not exasperate your children; instead, bring them up in the training and instruction of the Lord."[21]

God gives authority to parents, but with that authority comes responsibility. A father's role is not to rule with an iron first or abuse his position. Fathers and mothers are expected to be kind and compassionate, and even-handed. They are to train children in the instruction of the Lord, not their own whims or wishes. Godly training is what keeps families unified and cohesive. It creates a sense of vision and harmony within the family unit, and gives everyone a sense of purpose and commitment. Strong families are built on strong values. And it's a parent's job to instill and teach those values to their children.

The psalmist wrote, "How good and pleasant it is when God's people live together in unity!"[22]

God places a high premium on unity, because without it, the devil has a lot of opportunity to divide and conquer us. Disunity creates a sense of competition and restlessness. It creates discord among people who should be working toward the same goal and purpose.

Just Like Baking a Cake

In our kitchen pantry, we have all the ingredients to bake a chocolate cake. My wife could pull out everything she needs to make a delicious cake and put it all side by side on the counter. She'd pull out flour and sugar, baking soda, milk, eggs, cocoa, vegetable oil, and any other ingredients she might need.

She could put all these ingredients on the counter, but that doesn't make them a cake. Divided, they are just a handful of baking staples taking up space on the kitchen counter. There isn't much rhyme or reason for them to be there. If you put a spoonful of flour in your mouth it wouldn't taste very good. Sugar by itself would taste way too sweet, and cocoa would just be bitter.

But mix all of these ingredients together and you have a great tasting chocolate cake. They come together to make something much more special and appetizing than any of them could be on their own. In unity, they find their purpose.

The same is true for a family. When a family is divided, you have different people living under the same roof, each going their own way, each with their own idea about what they want to do and be, but not having much to do with the rest of the group. They may live together in the same house, but you could hardly call them a family. They are just individual ingredients, living side-by-side on the counter of life.

But mix them all together with a shared vision and goals and they suddenly become something beautiful and appetizing and special. They become something much greater and more fulfilling than any of them could have been on their own.

When everyone in the family is tuned to "Concert A," they are suddenly able to create beautiful music together.

In unity, they find their purpose as a family.

Unity in a Blended Family

Unity is important in all families, but especially critical in a blended family. When two families come together under one roof, there is likely a lot of mistrust and apprehension already built into the mix. People have been wounded before by people they trusted, and they're afraid of getting hurt again.

A young girl who feels betrayed and abandoned by her biological father is almost always going to struggle to trust another man to be a father to her. She will likely be reserved and reticent, unwilling to let her guard down again. She may cling to her mother and keep her stepfather at arm's length, just to keep her heart from getting hurt.

A young boy who watched his parents break up and go their separate ways will always wonder if the same thing might happen in his new family. On the surface he may seem fine, but inside he remains distant and skeptical. His mother may notice that he has become shy and reserved, but in reality, he is simply holding his emotions close to his chest. His defenses are up, because he feels the need to protect his family from more harm.

Teenagers in blended families often become openly rebellious and disobedient. They begin acting out in ways that they never have before. When they do, it's usually a defense mechanism. They are afraid of getting close, because they did that once only to be wounded and betrayed.

The dynamics involved in a blended family are almost always more difficult to navigate than a traditional family, because trust has not yet been established. That's why it is so important for parents to build a united front, and to work to bring everyone together under a shared vision and purpose. The parents' relationship to each other sets the tone and example for the entire family. When they are unified, the children will naturally begin to feel more secure and safe.

Disunity is what caused their previous family to fall apart. So unity is what they most need from the new one in order to trust again.

Unity Takes Effort

Building unity in a blended family takes an intentional level of effort and determination. It doesn't happen naturally. It takes time, patience, and purposeful conversations in order to create an air of trust among siblings and stepsiblings. Trust is a precious commodity that has to be sown and tended in order to grow. And trust is something you earn, not something you can demand.

The first step in building trust is developing a strong sense of belonging among every member of the family. You have to be physically and emotionally invested in each other's lives. You generate a sense of caring and camaraderie in the family by getting to know what's going on in each other's lives, and by fostering an attitude of love and solidarity.

And that is done by creating purposeful times of bonding and connection within the family.

Last weekend, my wife and I (Frank) were invited to a birthday dinner at the home of our daughter's new in-laws. They are one of the healthiest, closest families we know, and when you spend an evening with them, you begin to understand why.

There are five children in the family, three of whom are married, and two with children of their own, so it was a large gathering. We all squeezed together around a huge table filled with enough food to feed a small army. After praying over the meal, the kids started passing bowls of food around the table, each one filling their plate, then passing the bowls to the left. It was a seamless ritual that you could tell they had done a thousand times. All the while everyone was laughing and joking and having a merry time.

A few minutes into the meal, Dan, the father, got everyone's attention and said, "Okay, it's time to tell your one thing."

He explained to my wife and me that whenever they get together as a family, everyone has to share one important thing that happened to them during the previous week. I later learned that they had been doing this at mealtimes since the kids were very young.

As we ate, each person at the table took turns sharing something special that had happened to them during the previous week. One had been given an important new project at work, and they all congratulated her. Another had taken the first steps toward starting a new business, and they all encouraged him to stay at it. The oldest son had been able to share Jesus with a friend that week, and everyone was thrilled at the news. They all committed to praying for his friend during the coming week. It was one of the most encouraging family meals I'd ever attended, yet to them it was just a regular mealtime.

My wife and I are thrilled to have this wonderful family as our new in-laws, because they share all of our important values and beliefs. And they clearly know how to create a spirit of unity and togetherness within a large family. It's easy to see why their children are still best friends with each other, even though most have left home and started families of their own. There is a strong sense of oneness and caring among the siblings, and that doesn't happen by accident.

Ideas for Fostering Unity

There are many ways to generate a sense of love and unity within a family, whether it is a traditional or a blended one, but you have to actively work to make them happen.

Family traditions are great ways to help everyone bond. Our family has a number of holiday traditions that we practice each year, and it wouldn't feel like Thanksgiving or Christmas without them.

Family vacations can be invaluable for creating shared memories and experiences. But that doesn't happen unless you intentionally plan times to get away with the family, and make sure that everyone goes. And, you can involve the entire family in the planning process.

A weekly family night is another way to create times of bonding and unity. I know one family that has a pizza party every Friday night. They order pizza and choose a family-friendly movie to watch, and every member of the family has to be there. The kids can invite all the friends they like, and can request their favorite pizza, but they can't make other plans. It is a non-negotiable time of fun and fellowship. When their kids were very young, it was usually just a weekly family event, but today it has grown into a huge Friday night gathering among the kids' friends. Once a week, their house turns into the most happening place in the city, and the kids love it. Today they wouldn't dream of being anywhere but home on Friday evenings.

When it comes to creating times of bonding and unity in your family, ideas are plentiful. It just takes a little imagination and creativity, and a willingness to put them into practice. But the payoff is worth any effort you have to put into it.

We encourage you to do just that, and sooner, rather than later. When it comes to bringing your family together, there is no time better than the present.

Chapter
twenty

Strong Families Are Consistent

Every day couples stand before a minister at the altar and pledge their undying love for each other. They gaze into each other's eyes and promise to stay together through thick and thin. They are convinced that their love will never wane or falter, no matter what life throws in their path. They are fully infatuated, and are certain that nothing will ever change that.

Then a few years later they find themselves sitting in that same minister's office with their jaws clenched and their arms folded across their chests. He's convinced that he married the devil's sister, and she thinks he's the most obstinate and uncaring man to ever walk the earth. They are headed for divorce because they can't stand the sight of each other.

And the minister is thinking, "How in the world did this happen?"

I (Jimmy) have seen this scenario more times than you can imagine. And I've been in that minister's shoes. I've married couples that I knew in my heart were highly compatible, only to find myself helping them to repair their strained and damaged relationship a few years later.

Emotions Can't be Trusted

Too many people get married because they're convinced they've "fallen in love," only to later learn that falling out of love is just as easy. Their love was based on emotion, and emotions can't be trusted. A relationship built on emotions is both unstable and undependable.

Our emotions change by the day—sometimes by the hour. And feelings are driven by circumstance. When circumstances change, our emotions change with them. When life is going well and everyone is getting along, our emotions are steady and pleasant. But when something bad happens, our emotions suddenly take a nosedive. Within a matter of minutes, we can be depressed, angry, or in a state of shock.

A love built on emotions will be constantly changing and teetering depending on the circumstance of the moment. And that kind of love is destined to fail. Not likely to fail, but guaranteed to fail. It has absolutely no chance of survival.

You can't build a marriage on that kind of love, and you certainly can't sustain a family on it. For love to survive, it has to be a completely different kind of love. It has to be "agape" love.

Agape love is the kind of love that God has for you and me. It is based on decision, not emotion. God doesn't love us because we deserve it, but because He has decided to love. He has determined to be faithful and true to us, no matter what we do. His love for us is resolute and un-changing and consistent. It is an act of the will, not the emotions.

And that is the kind of love that He expects us to extend to others. We are to love each other with agape love. We decide to love, even when we don't feel loving. Love has to come from the will, not the emotions. And nowhere is this kind of love more critical than in the context of mar-riage and family.

Someone might ask me, "Jimmy, are you going to love Karen tomor-row?"

If I answer based on my emotions, the only answer I can give is, "I honestly don't know." Because I have no idea what might happen be-tween now and tomorrow. She might do something to make me furious. Or maybe she'll just wake up tomorrow in a bad mood. If my love is based on emotion, any of these things can affect my feelings for her. Every time circumstances change, my love will change with it. I can no more predict my emotions than I can predict the lottery, because emo-tions are fickle and fleeting and always changing.

But my love for Karen is not based on emotions. It is agape love. I have determined to love her. And because of that, I can answer without question or hesitation, "Of course I will love her tomorrow! There will never be a day in my life when I don't love Karen. She is the most beautiful and desirable woman in the world to me, and that will never change, no matter how old we get. I will love her until the day I die."

I can say that without reserve because my love for Karen is not based on anything she does or anything that might happen between us. It isn't based on emotions. It is agape love. I have chosen to love Karen. I have determined it as an act of my will, not my emotions.

God's Agape Love

If you have set out to build a happy and healthy blended family, the greatest thing you can do for your spouse, children and stepchildren is to love them with agape love. To determine to love them, no matter what happens, and no matter how they act. You decide to love them, no matter how obstinate or unlovable they choose to become.

You have to settle in your heart that you will love them regardless of how you feel toward them at a given moment. You love them whether they succeed or fail, whether they honor or embarrass you, whether they treat you with kindness or contempt. You love them when they deserve it, and love them when they don't. You even love them when you don't like them very much.

You choose to be steady and consistent and loving, no matter how you feel, or how circumstances may shift and change. The Bible tells us, "For God so loved the world that He gave His one and only Son, that whoever believes in Him shall not perish but have eternal life."[23]

I'm convinced that God doesn't always like the world. You and I have given Him a million reasons not to enjoy being around us. If God's love were based on emotions He would have likely turned us all in a big pile of dust by now. We disrespect Him. We ignore Him. We disobey Him. We defy Him. We take Him for granted. We disrespect His holiness. And it breaks His heart when we do that.

But His love for us never changes, because His love is agape love. It is a decision of the will. And it will never change.

Loving the Unlovable

I (Frank) know a couple who have a decidedly unlovable son. He is unable to care for himself because of a crippling disease he contracted at birth, so he still lives at home with his parents. He is cross and obstinate much of the time, and often lashes out at them for no reason. The boy is angry at the world and angry with God because of his disability, and it affects every aspect of his personality. But his parents continue to love him, no matter how he acts. They understand his frustration, and are committed to staying by his side, no matter what. They have shown tremendous patience toward their son, in spite of his unlovable disposition.

They do this because they have chosen to love him. They see the woundedness in his spirit, and have decided to extend a great deal of grace because of his pain. And their hope is that someday he will get past his pain and come back into relationship with God. So they treat him with the love and compassion he needs, not the way they might feel like treating him.

Their son has given them many reasons to turn their backs on him. Many parents in their position might have done that long ago, but their love is not based on emotion. It is a decision of their will. And they will love him regardless of whether he ever reciprocates.

If you are in a blended family, you are likely dealing with a lot of pain and wounds from past relationships. Your spouse may be struggling to get past some deeply-hidden inner vows from a past marriage. Your children may be harboring feelings of anger or doubt or shame. Your stepchildren may be having trouble accepting you as their new parent, and may be acting out in ways that seem unbearable.

You may need more patience than you think you can summon in order to navigate the family dynamics. If so, the only healthy response is to love them with agape love. You have to decide to show love, even when you don't feel like it. In spite of how they act and react toward you. Regardless of whether they ever choose to reciprocate your love.

You have to love them, even when you don't like them very much.

From God's Heart to Ours

That's a lot easier said than done. It's extremely difficult to love someone unconditionally when your love is not a two-way street. I don't have the strength in me to show consistent and deliberate love to someone who seems determined to take that love for granted, and you likely don't either. So how exactly are we supposed to summon the kind of agape love for others that God expects us to extend?

The answer is, you and I have to find a Source greater than ourselves to keep us filled. And only the well of God's love is deep enough to do that for us.

The Bible says, "We love because He first loved us."[24]

God's love is like a spring that never runs dry. And if we want to share that love with others, we have to be securely tapped into it. We have to be filled with God's love before we can extend that love to others.

Paul said, "God's love has been poured out into our hearts through the Holy Spirit, who has been given to us."[25]

When you and I accepted Jesus as our Lord and Savior, God sent the Holy Spirit to dwell within us. The same Spirit that lived in Jesus now lives in us. The agape love that flowed through God's heart now flows into and through ours, and by the power of the Holy Spirit, that love can now flow out to others.

God's love is already in us. As Christians, it has become part of our DNA. Loving unconditionally is not just something we do; it is who we are in Christ. It is our identity as followers of Jesus, and should flow through us as readily as God's love flows to us.

And nowhere should that be more apparent than in the way we act at home, among those who most need to feel loved.

Consistent Love

Healthy families are consistent families. Their love for each other isn't ruled by emotions or swayed by the circumstance of the moment. It doesn't change with the passing of time, or shift with the changing of the seasons. It is deliberate, decisive, and unwavering. It is an act of the will, not a byproduct of the emotions.

There are a lot of challenges involved in growing a strong and healthy stepfamily. There are personality conflicts to navigate, financial hurdles to overcome, deep wounds that still need healing, and damaged and battered emotions that can easily rise to the surface. At times, the struggles can feel overwhelming. During those times, what your family most needs is a beacon of love and consistency that stands tall and true, regardless of the winds or storms that come against it. They need to know that no matter what happens, no matter how tough life gets, or how scary the storms become, you will be there, steadily shining through the gale-force winds and guiding them to safe waters.

They need a rock to hang onto in times a trouble. A constant and steady anchor in an unpredictable and insecure world.

Your family should be bored by how consistently loving and dependable you are. It should so much a part of your character and personality that they don't even notice it anymore. Your unconditional love for them should be so ingrained in your relationship that they come to take it for granted.

That's when you'll know you're doing it right.

Love your family with God's agape love, and no trial or struggle can ever tear you apart. Not even the challenges of building a strong, happy, and healthy blended family.

Endnotes

1   See Malachi 2:16

2   Romans 3:23

3   1 John 1:9

4   See Hebrews 8:12

5   See Psalm 103:12

6   Romans 8:1

7   Mark 10:7-8

8   Ephesians 4:26-27

9   2 Corinthians 10:3-5

10   Matthew 6:12

11   Matthew 6:14-15

12   Luke 6:27-28,31

13   Luke 6:27-28

14   Gottman, John. "John Gottman on Trust and Betrayal." 29 Oct. 2011. Greater Good. April 15, 2015 www.greatergood.berkeley.edu

15   James 1:19-20

16   Amos 3:3 (NKJV)

17   Proverbs 11:14 (NASB)

18   Matthew 22:37-40

19   Isaiah 53:2-3

20   Ephesians 6:1-3

21   Ephesians 6:4

22   Psalm 133:1

23   John 3:16

24   1 John 4:19

25   Romans 5:5